What successful coaches in  are saying about The Mind's Eye...

"For the serious coach who is looking for an additional edge in his coaching 'toolkit', **The Mind's Eye** is a must read. Passages and techniques in this book brought back memories in the skills of mental training in flow by my late coaches Neil Campbell, Stan Murdza and Bill Dick. Techniques and ideals that I still use today as a coach. I have just completed my third read of this book and will refer to it many times for the betterment of my athletes."

Ron Swede Burak
Varsity Lightweight Women's Rowing Coach
Brock University, St. Catherines, Canada

Throughout his coaching career, Jimmy Joy has sought to integrate philosophical and psychological insights with physical training. His concept of "Flow" stresses the importance of technique and swing in rowing, as well as the essential unity of mind, body and spirit in the successful athlete. His new book, **The Mind's Eye**, is a must-read for both rowing enthusiasts and students of coaching methods.

Art Wilmarth
Yale Oarsmen, Class of 1972
Professor of Law, George Washington University

"A manual for training the athlete's body, mind, and spirit that should be required for coaches in not only rowing, but all sports."

Mark Davis
Head Coach of Men's Rowing
George Washington University, USA

"Jim Joy has written a comprehensive, easy-to-use book that emphasizes the value of mental training for coaches and athletes at any level. It contains practical, step-by-step guides for specific implementation of his program in any training cycle. **The Mind's Eye** is a resource that will be useful for those who've employed mental training practices for years, or for those who've shied away from it because they may not have known where to begin."

Stew Stokes
Head Coach of Rowing
Colby College, USA

"For the rowers in the reading audience, be prepared to be challenged about what you think you know about the sport...This is a book that can point you in a new direction."

Mike Thompson
Canadian National Team Rowing Coach

"I loved the book! I really enjoyed how Jim brought together teachings from so many coaches and scholars."

Becky Robinson
Head Women's Rowing Coach
Ithaca College, USA

"A must read for "all" coaches and instructors. Most athletes get little or no mental training. The mental side of athletics separate the ordinary from the extraordinary athletes. This book will give your athletes (in all sports) an edge and raises the bar for coaches and their athletes."

Len De Francesco
Assistant Tennis Coach
William Smith College, USA

"**The Mind's Eye** presents a complete overview of the topic of Integral Coaching and the Focus of the Rower. It is wonderful to read his complete thoughts on this subject, since I know he presented only parts of it in *Rowing Faster*. He makes the whole topic flow from one important argument to the next and gives wonderful examples for coaches and athletes. Someone who reads this book should get incredible ideas what they can do to improve their rowing and their coaching. In addition, Jim's ideas are also a philosophy of rowing, training and coaching. It is wonderful to read and see difference of his approach contrasted to the many negative examples that we see with the "winning at all cost" philosophy. If people will take these ideas, rowing will become a better sport than it is already!"

Dr. Volker Nolte
Assistant Professor & Men's Rowing Coach
University of Western Ontario, Canada

THE MIND'S EYE

Additional Resources by Jimmy Joy

Books
COMING SOON! *The Slide World: The Dynamic Technique of Sculling and Rowing*

Articles
The Run of the Shell

Effortless Power

Body Awareness and Movement Training

Relaxation and Movement

Training for Flow

Beginner to Advanced Movement/Technique

Integral Coaching

Rowing Drills

Conference
The Joy of Sculling Coaching Conference

To learn more about these references please visit www.joyofsculling.com

THE MIND'S EYE

The Evolution of the Athlete's Skills and Consciousness

Jimmy Joy

The Joy of Sculling
Geneva, NY

Joy of Sculling

Published by James C. Joy
P.O. Box 567
Geneva, New York 14456
Phone: (315) 781-2383
Email: joyofsculling@mac.com
Website: www.thejoyofsculling.com

Cover Design by Kit Casey

Second Edition Revised and Expanded, June 2010

Dedication

To my sculling coach, Bob Fitzpatrick of Halifax, Nova Scotia and to my wrestling coach, Dr. Michael Yuhasz of London, Ontario.

Both were masters of Flow and Integration.

Joy of Sculling

Foreword

When you first meet Jimmy Joy, you can't be but impressed with his warm, interpersonal style. He is energetic but reserved, welcoming and definitely not intimidating – although he might be! Lurking behind that ready smile and twinkling eye is a brain ever ready for new ideas, ever ready to share with you. Very early on, Jim began to quietly challenge me as to what I thought about our common passion, rowing. Our ways parted for some time, and it took until the reading of this book for me to discover from where Jim's thoughtfulness springs: the simple answer is "everywhere!"

One of Jim's passions is the concept of *flow* – that elusive element which is not easily attained and can separate the talented individual from the journeyman athlete. While I can't state definitively whether "flow" begat Jim's study of the inner athlete, or if it was the reverse, I can say that Jim's fresh approach to combining elements of mental conditioning with technical training that produce "flow" more consistently makes this book a necessary inclusion on the serious coach's bookshelf. You will quickly discover that Jim is widely-read, with his interests spanning philosophy, history, and a philosophical-historical approach to coaching. One would have to read through a library full of books to find a volume which combines Eknath Easwaran with Phil Jackson – and be unsuccessful in your search!

We are all the product of our life experiences – Jimmy's makes him uniquely qualified to author The Mind's Eye. Applying the techniques of this book will help you and your athletes to better performances, and will produce a legacy of consciousness for life – if the experiences of Jimmy's athletes at Yale and Hobart William Smith Colleges are any indication. Jimmy's account of Integral Coaching brings the reader to the realization that the philosophical approach to mental conditioning is wholly practical, and the coach assumes the role of informed educator: the highest level of coaching, which transcends sport, and serves to prepare the individual for more than just racing, in my mind.

For the rowers in the reading audience, be prepared to be challenged about what you think you know about the sport, your perceptions of the sport, and your overall approach to rowing and sculling. For those who do not share our passion for the oar, read on! This is a book that can point you in a new direction and challenge your current perceptions and beliefs in any sport or activity. Jim has masterfully combined his philosophy with practical examples from his very successful coaching career to produce a singularly unique read. While you may not be motivated to check out your local rowing club after you put the book down, you are bound to find a new view on the challenge of optimal performance which has been hanging around for a while. Either way, your life is about to be enhanced for the better. I know you will enjoy The Mind's Eye as much as I did!

Mike Thompson
Canadian National Team Coach
St. Catherines, Ontario
November 1, 2009

Acknowledgements

First, I would like to acknowledge my wife Cecilia, for her love, support, and encouragement for this project that she has provided throughout the years. I am also grateful to my daughter, Christina, as well as Gail Burr, Tom Weil and Jon Van Amringe for their editing contributions throughout various stages of the book's development. I appreciate Art Wilmarth's contribution on *Flow*, along with John Ossowski's and Amy Wettergreen's accounts of their *Flow* experiences. In addition, special friends, and educators, Terry and Beverly McKinney of Buckhorn, Ontario, and former Yale lightweight oarsmen Van Amringe, Art Wilmarth, and Tom Weil, have been invaluable sources of support and encouragement for my coaching and writing over many years.

The coaching aspect of the topic really began with my Yale students from 1966 to 1972 and reached a high level of sophistication with the Hobart and William Smith students from 1989 to 1999. During the 1990s, my numerous trips to Japan provided a lasting image of dedicated and focused sculling by Coach Max Suzuki's students from the National College of Physical Education. Some went on to row and scull with the National team. They were clearly at a higher level of skill and consciousness. As coaches we must live the life that we share with our athletes, family and good friends. All of these people represent an important component in completing this book, and I want them to know how integral and important they are to me and my life.

Also, I thank Coach Michael Thompson for his generous and insightful foreword to the book. Other coaches on this wonderful odyssey who deserve recognition for their influence and guidance include the late Jack McAleese and Bob Fitzpatrick of St. Catharines, my university coaches in football and wrestling, Jack Fairs and Dr. Michael Yuhasz respectively, former USA National Team Coaches Jim Barker and Allen Rosenberg, the late James Rathschmidt of Yale, the late Joe Burk at Penn, Canadian National Team Coaches Boris Klavora, the late Neil Campbell, Jack Nicholson, Ted Daigenault, Dick McClure, Ed McNeely, Al Morrow, Volker Nolte, Mike Spracklen, and from abroad, Penny Chuter of Great Britain, the late Ivan Vanier of the Netherlands, Thor Nilsen of Norway and Dr. Theo Korner of the DDR.

Finally, I thank Nich Lee for his skilled collaboration and patience as my editor and for his tireless efforts in formatting and managing the other requirements that come with publishing a book.

Jimmy Joy
June 2010

The Old Coach

"The human potential is infinitely greater than we have been led to believe."

George Leonard

Robert Fitzpatrick of Canada, an excellent sculling coach, encouraged his athletes to visualize the stroke cycle by using "the Mind's Eye." He simply meant that the athlete should try to create a mental image of the stroke cycle. Initially, this was difficult for his athletes to grasp, but it did come easier over the years because his coaching incorporated meditative practices into the skill training. This combinination of consciousness and technical training advanced not only the athlete's understanding of the specific movements of the stroke, but also the ability to execute them effectively. Fitzpatrick's approach developed mental confidence, self-knowledge, and a relaxed, economical, and fluid stroke action.

Fitzpatrick also encouraged his athletes to observe the smooth body action of athletes from other sports. This practice established the habit of watching and appreciating precision timing, effortless movement, fluid swings, and throws or strides of other athletes. Consequently, the athlete came to recognize the economy of effort as a common thread between all sports and all accomplished athletes. Athletes exhibiting this dynamic and effortless motion in the 1950s and 1960s included: Sir Stanley Mathews and Pele in soccer, John Landy and Herb Elliot in running, Don Scholander in swimming, Gordie Howe with his easy stride in hockey, Ted Williams with his fluid swing in baseball, Ivanov, the three-time Olympic gold medalist in the single scull, and the American football star, Jimmy Brown. These same fluid movements can be observed in athletes today. We simply have to look for them.

Other great coaches have used similar approaches in studying movement. Percy Cerutty, the Australian track coach, encouraged his athletes to observe the fluidity of dogs and cats, the ease of flight of birds, the effortless movements of fish and the endless, relaxed, endurance of young children. Similarly, Barry Lopez in his wonderful book, *Arctic Deams*, lavished praise on the athleticism and fluid movements of the polar bear. It is also helpful to study the percision of esteemed dancers, including: Fred Astaire, Gene Kelly, Dame Margot Fonteyn, Rudolph Nureyev and Mikhail Nikolaevich Baryshnikov. While these dancers move fluidly on the stage, the essence of the sculler's movements is to similarly dance and flow in the shell. Kelly made an excellent documentary in 1958 titled *Dancing: A Man's Game*, in which he demonstrated the moves of various outstanding athletes as forms of dance movements. He used Sugar Ray Robinson from boxing, Vic Seixias from Tennis, Mickey Mantle from baseball and Dick Button from figure skating as his models. Gene Kelly was a great beliver in the solid connection between his own athleticism and dance.

In daily practice, dancers and figure skaters epitomize the complete athlete. Their training is holistic and very thorough, encompassing a wide range of activities including visualization, concentration, relaxation and strength training. Interestingly, Fitzpatrick was an avid observer of the Radio City Rockettes and professional skaters, citing them often for their flawless precision.

His advice of looking for this quality in other athletes reinforced the intensive, focused training for flow in the boat. Under Fitzpatrick's carefully planned guidance, this quality of fluid movement permeated one's consciousness and awareness. The objective of training was the smooth, efficient body action that linked your will and your spirit for learning with your enjoyment for doing and performing the skill: the athlete evolved into a dedicated student and a skilled practitioner of sculling. You were "either a sculler or a slugger." The intelligence of the sculler speaks through his hands. When the athlete flows, he becomes a sculler and achieves his best possible performance. On the other hand, when the slugger struggles with the movements, he often underperforms. Fitzpatrick's coaching enhanced the athlete's evolving consciousness of the link between total body awareness and the relaxed stroke. He was a pioneer in this psychological dimension of coaching, recognizing the importance of mental training as the foundation for the optimal development of the athlete.

Fortunately for me, Fitzpatrick's summer emphasis on flow and integration was augmented during the winter months by Dr. Michael Yuhasz, my university wrestling coach. Yuhasz, like Fitzpatrick, engaged in mastery training in which the athlete learned a few skills well before moving to the next level of skill training. Yuhasz also stressed the need for flow between your various moves. So, it was a fluid transition from the water's sculling skills of balance, economy and timing, to the similar demands of wrestling.

Fitzpatrick used the meditative practices described in the following pages to develop the mind and body. He was subtle in weaving the mind training into the fabric of the skills practice. For example, his training of the trunk swing timing took miles and miles of concentrated sculling. In the end however, his methods produced an extremely effective motion — an effortless glide forward in combination with an acute feel for the run of the shell run. This development occured when the instincts became more acute, which was a direct result of his integrated coaching. The sculling became part of your being, and as he stated, the feeling and timing of the swing would remain with you forever, and it did. I should add however, that the terminology and actual practice of Fitzpatrick's various meditative methods were not as sophisticated or detailed as outlined here.

In addition to mental training, Fitzpatrick also believed strongly in the effectiveness of stroke simulation exercises. These drills were advantageous in developing the timing of individual movements and the timing of a crew as a whole. During the winter months these exercises were performed on the rowing machine or in a rowing tank without the use of the machine handle or the oar. Years later an excited sports psychologist informed me that the simulation exercises were excellent "pump primers" for visualization. In fact, the simulation exercises were an elaborate form of concentration training.

Looking back, my association with Fitz was a wonderful 15 year odyssey of movement learning, mental conditioning and subtle skills training. It was clearly Fitzpatrick's intention to connect skill development with the evolution of an expansive consciousness. His subtle insertion of mental practices into the training accelerated the muscle/ mind process resulting in a knowledgeable, efficient athlete. Without this integration it may take multiple early sport experiences and years of practice for the athlete to reach a high level of proficiency. Coaches who can properly and successfully integrate mental training with their athletes will see highly efficient athletes who generate consistent performances. Fitzpatrick undersood this.

The following pages contain a portion of his teaching in order that coaches and athletes may experience Fitzpatrick's methods for integrating the athlete's consciousness and skills, as taught to and learned by more than a thousand athletes over my coaching career.

Joy of Sculling

An Introduction to Consciousness

"To practice quieting and focusing your mind, it's usually quite helpful to quiet and relax your body and your environment to begin with. When you get good at it, you can practice meditation on the New York subway...So the general instructions for teaching people concentrative meditation are first, get in a quiet place...The second part of quieting your environment is to reduce the time pressure of a hurried, scheduled life."

Charles Tart

Fitz's method of integrated skill and consciousness training optimized the development of relaxation and focusing. He utilized five types of meditative practice to develop consciousness, or a complete awareness of one's surroundings: quiet sitting, visualization, relaxation, concentration, and mindfulness. To have a relaxed focus on race day involves lengthy, patient and systematic training by the athlete and coach.* This partnership requires

---

* Self-Test: Were you patient enough to read through the quote at the beginning of the chapter, or did you jump straight to the first sentence? Patience and Consciousness is critical for coaching.

both parties to work intensively together. Over time, the consistent reinforcement of relaxing and focusing becomes very evident in the accuracy and effectiveness of the racing stroke, and in the improvement of the athlete's training and overall performance.

The inherent message of merging the athlete's skills with his inner state easily applies to other symmetrical sports, such as running, swimming, skiing and cycling. Rowing can also use the lessons of coaches from these repetitive pattern sports who have combined the mental and physical skills in their coaching. Track coach Percy Cerutty of Australia and Phil Jackson of basketball fame, who I discuss later in this book, are two prominent examples of coaches to study.

In the 1990s Michael Jordan's playing demonstrated that indeed, mental training optimizes the potential performance level of the individual athlete. Coach Phil Jackson expressed a similar line of thought in his admiration of the NBA star. "In the process of becoming a great athlete Michael has attained a quality of mind few Zen students ever achieve. His ability to stay relaxed and intensely focused in the midst of chaos is unsurpassed."[1]

Table 1.1 on the following page illustrates an overview of the periodization scheme for planning the five stages of mental training. It should be noted that the ability to sit quietly (quiet sitting) is the foundation for the other meditative practices used throughout the year that enable exceptional performances. It is always beneficial for resetting the

---

[1] Phil Jackson, *Sacred Hoops: Spiritual Lessons of a Hardwood Warrior* (New York, NY: Hyperion, 1995).

organism to sit quietly before practices, races and championships. To this end, Fitzpatrick would have the athlete sit quietly for a few minutes of reflection before doing a practice piece. This resetting the body and mind is more likely to produce a better training session. Also, this resetting of the body for optimal performance can be achieved prior to practice and racing through massage, yoga, flexibility training and the other meditative practices.

Table 1.1 The Annual Cycle of Mental Training

SEP	OCT	NOV	DEC	JAN	FEB	MAR	APR	MAY	JUN	JUL	AUG
Quiet Sitting											
Visualization	Relaxation		Mindfulness						Concentration		
				Visualization		Concentration		Visualization			

The integral approach to training highlights the importance of cross training, including hill and long distance running, jumping rope and the all important yoga for flexibility. The ability to remain in the moment, to experience heightened mental awareness and to appreciate the connection with your environment illustrate just a few of the benefits athletes and coaches derive from quietly relaxing and focusing in many physical training situations, not just rowing. The focus learned to keep jumping rope after fatigue sets in expands and strengthens the mind, while ultimately aiding the ability to stay focused near the end of a race or a long practice.

During my time coaching, I found that meditative practices accelerated the depth and scope of my self knowledge, and ultimately, had a positive effect on my coaching development. My athletes felt similarly after experiencing the program described in this book. As evidence, one evening shortly after I had retired from coaching at William Smith College, a number of my former students visited my home. During our ensuing conversation they said that it was fine for me to share technique, training methods, and physiological testing information with other schools. However, they were adamant that I withhold the information pertaining to the design and implementation of our mental training program. They felt that this component was the edge they had enjoyed over their competition. It provided consistency in their performance as the meditation produced a consistant mental state that was projected to the body. Bebe Bryans, the Georgetown women's rowing coach at the time, recognized this quality in the William Smith crews at the 1996 championship regatta when she shook my hand and congratulated me on the crews' consistent performances over the years.

Unfortunately, Fitzpatrick did not have a workout venue available to him over the winter training period, so he curtailed the use of the meditative practices to the on-water workouts. However, in my coaching, I developed and expanded these practices throughout the year in accordance with the time frame illustrated in Table 1.1. Consequently, the winter months, with a controlled indoor environment, presented an excellent opportunity to introduce and do concentrated practices. The use of the five meditative practices became routine and part of the fabric of the total training program. Completing these exercises on a regular basis developed a natural progression from quiet sitting, to mindfulness, to *flow* and peak performance.

The mental state of the athlete in this process becomes part of her evolution to a deeper, more complete being. Sri Aurobindo, the great Indian philosopher of the 20th century, wrote, " We might say, there are two beings in us, one on the surface, our exterior mind, life, body consciousness, and another behind the veil, an inner mind, an inner life, an inner physical consciousness constituting another or inner self."[2] At times we have all experienced the feeling of power coming from our inner self especially when our athletic body has been finely tuned through proper training, careful attention to nutrition, and regenerative rest. This is the ultimate challenge for the coach and athlete — to exploit the athlete's deeper and more powerful resources.

Although these meditative exercises have practical value for athletes and coaches, they remain misunderstood or underappreciated by most of the sports world. Possibly this is changing, as witnessed by the success of Phil Jackson's efforts with the Chicago Bulls and now with the Los Angeles Lakers. However, Jackson does enjoy an advantage over his coaching colleagues from his seeking and familarizing himself with the teachings of the various spiritual masters when he was a young coach. As proof, a former athlete of Jackson characterizes

---

[2] Sri Aurobindo, *The Integral Yoga: Sri Aurobindo's Teaching and Method of Practice - Selected Letters of Sri Aurobindo* (Twin Lakes, WI: Lotus Light Publications, 1993).

communication with him as a "form of meditation."[3] With this meditative approach coaches and athletes will ultimately realize the accessibilty of more power internally.

In the final stages of this study, the objective becomes the investigation of effective body movement, or a more organic motion instead of a merely mechanical one. This includes the study of the "flow" phenomenon. If consciousness is an awareness of one's self and surroundings, then *flow* is an advanced state of consciousness which expands the mind beyond visual and physical boundaries. It is a state in which the effortless swing, stride or stroke simply exists. It involves the total integration of the inner self, the body, and the environment in which boundaries disappear. This produces effective shell run.

You can experience and simulate this "no boundary state" when you close your eyes during quiet sitting. In that moment all that you can directly feel is the slight pressure on your backside as the organism melts into the surrounding environment. With the eyes closed you begin to "sense" the world around instead of just seeing it. This is a clear and distinct experience of our organism extending beyond your skin and a recognition that you are more than your body. You are part of a seamless, larger world. The challenge lies in finding a similar relationship with your immediate environment when the eyes are open.

To recognize that our immediate surroundings and the larger universe are alive and part of you requires a much different mental framework and a

---

[3] Jackson, *Sacred Hoops: Spiritual Lessons of a Hardwood Warrior.*

lowering of the ego levels. The mind should not be intense, but rather expansive and encompassing. You begin to realize that the environment should be part of you and you should be part of the environment. Your powers of awareness require this development for a peak performance to occur. Duane Elgin, in his wonderfully insightful work, *The Living Universe*, brings our attention to the living universe philosophy and the impact on our potential:

> *"In a dead universe, the boundaries of our being are defined by the extent of our physical body. However, in a living universe, our physical existence is permeated and sustained by an aliveness that is inseparable from the aliveness of the universe. If we are beings whose consciousness can extend beyond our biological bodies and into the reaches of the living universe, then our physical bodies only comprise the smallest fraction of the full scope of our being."[4]*

As a coach I would have the athletes look at the trees located across the canal from the boathouse as an object and then reverse the situation by having the athletes imagine that they were the object and the trees the subject, which was looking at them. The goal was to expand the mind and make it more encompassing. Also, at the end of running hills for 25-30 minutes, the athletes would experience the sensation of grasping the trunk of a tree as an expression of their relating to nature. After one such early morning workout a couple of two-hundred

---

[4] Duane Elgin, *The Living Universe: Where Are We? Who Are We? Where Are We Going?* (San Francisco, CA: Berrett-Koehler, 2009).

pound athletes got my attention as they were doing a tandem hug on a huge maple tree; humor is valued and important for one's complete development. They had managed to integrate their sense of humor with their environmental display, while retaining respect for the underlying lesson.

For the ultimate *flow* state to occur, the coach, athlete and team must be fully integrated in all aspects of body, mind and spirit. Phil Jackson refers to this as the "power of we rather than the power of me."[5] When we speak of this power, it refers to both the individual and group actions as well as to the internal and external being. I witnessed this power in 1984 with coach Neil Campbell and the Canadian Olympic Gold Medal Eight. The Canadian eight of that year was a complete unit with a single spirit. This efficient body/mind/spirit state provides the necessary relaxation, concentration and focus for race day, and the ability to enjoy the competitive moment.

---

[5] Jackson, *Sacred Hoops: Spiritual Lessons of a Hardwood Warrior*.

The Process

"At the start of the season, the group had barely been able to watch five minutes of a game tape without getting so restless that they couldn't concentrate. Slowly, however, I was able to build up their endurance so that by the playoffs they were able to view entire ball games with full attention. Similarly I initially introduced them to three-minute periods of meditation and gradually stretched them out to ten minutes. After a while they were even willing to participate in yoga sessions. The constant practice of awareness and concentration certainly made the group easier to coach"

Phil Jackson

As mentioned previously, the training plan includes five types of meditative practices outlined in the following sections. These practices are integrated into the daily workout schedule, providing an effective use of time by the consolidation of the meditative and physical skills. The use of each meditative principle applies on the water, in the weight room or with any other type of training. In the early stages, the quiet sitting, relaxation and visualization practices are emphasized while concentration and mindfulness are added later. With this approach, the mental training becomes ordinary and fundamental, and is consequently viewed by the athlete as routine instead of something extra or separate from the physical and technical training. In fact, the physical and technical training provides the necessary focus for intensive mental training. During any mental training sessions on land the coach participates with the athlete and therefore reinforces the importance of this particular activity. When the athletes sit, he sits with them. The coach not only describes, but also models the practices by simultaneously working on his inner self.

To achieve a fully developed mental control of the self is extremely beneficial on race day. It allows the athlete and the coach to be relaxed and focused. Phil Jackson relates that it took him two years to convince the Chicago Bulls to do group meditation.[6] Jackson writes, "The first time we practiced meditation, Michael (Jordan) thought I was joking. Midway through the session, he cocked one eye open and took a glance around the room to see if any of his teammates were actually doing it. To his surprise, many of them were."[7] I had the same experience at Yale with the simulation exercises and at Hobart-William Smith with the meditative practices. In both situations it took two years for athletes to feel comfortable with themselves engaging in the practices.

An important byproduct of the team sitting together on a regular basis is the enhancement of the team concept (athletes and coaches) and group spirit. With regular daily practice, the athlete's powers of

---

[6] "Interview with Phil Jackson," (USA: CNN, 2002).

[7] Phil Jackson and Charles Rosen, *More Than a Game* (New York, NY: Seven Stories Press, 2001).

awareness and the ability to remain in the present moment increases dramatically. Everyone on the team comes to understand that there is a systematic method of mental training that is integrated with the technique training and physical training. The total process builds confidence in the individual and between team members.

Integration and wholeness are stressed and constantly reinforced throughout the training. These two concepts are critical for the proper execution of the stroke cycle. In order to foster this development of wholeness and integration, rowing by all eight should be stressed in place of rowing by pairs, fours or sixes, especially the closer you get to racing. The worst-case scenario took place at the IRA in the 1990's with a coxed four rowing to the start into a headwind by pairs with square blades. Honestly, what did this have to do with preparation for an important race in 15 minutes? Very little. In contrast, before a race at Lucerne, I witnessed an East German Women's Quad engaged in fast arm simulations before boating for their heat. The women were integrating a skill into their warmup routine that was directly related to their upcoming race. So, it is important to keep these two factors, integration and wholeness, always in mind, whether you are coaching a segment of the stroke cycle, observing their weight training or performing any aspect of the training plan.

Any visualization exercise aims to address many needs of the athlete both directly related to rowing and indirectly related to life. Remember that an athlete who can balance and manage the external forces affecting their training will ultimately experience better and more frequent training.

The remainder of this chapter is comprised of sections which elaborate on a specific meditative process. Included at the beginning of each section is a table containg information on how to employ the information to complement and enhance the physical training.

Quiet Sitting

*"Eventually I stir, roused by the haggle of ravens or the chatter
of squirrels or the scurry of deer — other minds in the forest —
and I make my way back along the trail to the zone of
electricity and words. As I walk, it occurs to me that meditation
is an effort to become for a spell more like a tree, open to
whatever arises, without judging, without remembering the
past or anticipating the future, fully present in the moment. The
taste of that stillness refreshes me. And yet I do not aspire to
dwell in such a condition always. For all its grandeur and
beauty, for all its half — millennium longevity, the Douglas Fir
cannot ponder me, cannot reflect or remember or imagine —
can only be. In so far as meditation returns us to a state of
pure unreflective being, it is a respite from the burden of
ceaseless thought. When we surface from the meditation,
however, we are not turning from reality to illusion, as some
spiritual traditions would have us believe, we are reclaiming
the full powers of mind, renewed by our immersion in the realm
of mountains and rivers, wind and breath."*

Scott Russell Sanders

How should meditative practices be
introduced? Meditation may appear foreign or strange
to coaches and athletes, although in most cases
people have encountered and perhaps engaged in
these practices, but not in any systematic manner.
Often the athletes and coaches are probably not even
aware of having had this experience. In a similar
fashion, athletes may not realize that the flexibilty
exercises that they perform religiously are derived
from yoga. Coaches should introduce meditation by
avoiding the word "meditation" and instead tell the
atletes to sit quietly on the floor with their legs
crossed in total stillness for three minutes. They will
almost undoubtedly, and without fail, readjust their
position, open their eyes or talk. After a few minutes

Table 2.1 Quiet Sitting	
Meditative Method on Land	• Relaxed posture • Sitting on floor • Eyes closed • Incorporate yoga style stretching
Meditative Method on Water	• Minimal talking from coach/cox • Maintain silence • Longer distance steady state rowing without any body tension
Practice Schedule on Land	• Practice 5x weekly at 3-5' per session • Yoga ~ 5-10' daily
Practice Schedule on Water	• Practice 10', 20' and 30' pieces in silence around 3x per week
Training Phase	• First month of preparatory phase • Throughout the year for 3-5' at the beginning and/or end of practice to slow down

let them know that they were unable to follow the instructions. Simply state that remaining still constitutes a key compenent for successful performances. If they can't sit quietly for three minutes in practice, how can they expect to perform multiple repetitions of the stroke without error in competition when their muscles are burning and their hearts are beating furiously? Explain to them that they are developing a quiet, unhurried, calm center in their being that will serve them well in their performances, in the classroom, and in life. The athlete's realization of the importance of the quiet and the stillness establishes the tone for all subsequent mental training practices because they have experienced the value of connecting their minds, their bodies, and their surroundings. In the ensuing days, the simplest and most effective instruction requires 3 to 5 minutes of quiet sitting at the beginning of each practice. The body posture remains informal at this stage. As they gain more practice the athletes assume a more erect sitting posture - straight back, crossed legs, head up and eyes open or closed. So, there is some added benefit for the athlete's lower core muscular development from the sittings. Allan Combs, in his extra-ordinary book, *The Radiance of Being*, quotes the late Tibetan master, Chogyam Trungpa, on the importance of good posture.

> *"In the practice of meditation, an upright posture is extremely important. Having an upright back is not an artificial posture. It is natural to the human. When you slouch, that is unusual. You can't breathe properly when you slouch."*[8]

Combs goes on to say that "This meditative posture moves the meditator toward a quiet and relaxed state of clarity...virtually all of the subtle states of consciousness require this silent clarity, and only the most advanced practitioner can carry it outward into ordinary day-to-day living."[9] This important characteristic of our dynamic body is a

-----

[8] Allan Combs, *The Radiance of Being: Complexity, Chaos, and the Evolution of Consciousness* (St. Paul, MN: Paragon House, 1996).

[9] Combs, *The Radiance of Being: Complexity, Chaos, and the Evolution of Consciousness*.

crucial factor in the shell for relaxation and for power application. You must have good posture — this is certainly reinforced through the quiet sitting. It is an important ingredient for the length and power of the stroke. The coach can illustrate the additional length with the elongated back position in contrast to the rounded back position by using his hand to simulate the reach positions, an extended hand contrasted to a cupped hand.

Good posture in and out of the shell was an important quality that Fitzpatrick stressed. He led by example because he maintained a relaxed posture, with a straight carriage and erect head, right to his death at the age of 81. Bill Bowerman, the legendary track coach at the University of Oregon, felt "that good posture was essential for good body mechanics" regardless of the time or place.[10] Consequently, I urge people to row their length, the natural length of their body gained through excellent posture, and I encourage athletes to be aware of their standing, sitting, walking and running positions. When driving a vehicle, check the rear view mirror at the beginning and end of the drive to verify that you have maintained your correct sitting position throughout the trip. You can remind yourself to sit erect when at your desk or on the computer. This emphasis on good posture also addresses the importance of core training in order to develop and maintain this erect posture.

As stated earlier, quiet sitting is an effective method by which the coach and the athlete integrate into a unit - if the coach sits with the team. This is

---

[10] William J. Bowerman, *High-Performance Training for Track and Field* (Champaign, IL: Leisure Press, 1991).

also an excellent example of leadership by imitation. By sitting regularly, the team, coaches and athletes, learn to be aware of the present moment by using various meditative supports, including physical feelings, sounds, small objects and counting breaths. For the more proficient practitioner, a lighted candle in a quiet room is an excellent method for individual practice. Then the only thing that you need to focus on is your internal quiet. The use of this particular practice is scheduled throughout the year. This quiet time is reinforced with an alternative approach of some concentrated stretching (yoga) combined with systematic breathing. By using the quiet sitting and yoga stretching we recognize the need to slow down from the fast pace of daily modern life. Eknath Easwaran, Indian philosopher and teacher, provided the following eight points for slowing down:

a. Get up early
b. Don't crowd your day
c. Ask "What is important?"
d. Take time for relationships
e. Take time for reflection
f. Don't let yourself get hurried
g. Respond with patience
h. Slow down the mind[11]

It should be noted that the last three pieces of Easwaren's advice are applicable to both practice and racing.

---

[11] Eknath Easwaran, *Meditation: A Simple Eight-Point Program for Translating Spiritual Ideals into Daily Life* (Tomales, CA: Nilgiri Press, 1991).

In addition to slowing down, the quiet sitting helps the team to experience the present moment; racing the course is the experience of stroke by patient stroke and moment by patient moment. This ability to remain in the present moment involves both relaxation and concentration. T.S. Eliot, highlights this quality of consciousness and the importance of remaining in the moment in his poetry, *Four Quartets*:

> *Time past and time future*
> *Allow but a little consciousnes*
> *To be conscious is not to be in time*[12]

Coaches and athletes should incorporate this concept of quiet sitting into the on water training by using long distance silent rows and concentrating on timing and technique. The only words spoken come from the coxswain, "let it run, turn around, ready, row." Phil Jackson employs this method by conducting whole practices in silence. He feels it develops the athlete's mindfulness. The use of slow motion rowing, either on the ergometer or on the water develops stillness, accuracy, and total awareness of the movements. My first use of slow motion occurred during my own sculling days when doing a long approach to the dock at the end of practice. The slow approach to the landing using my peripheral vision was a fun exercise in mindfulness, especially when some anxious bystander would rush to try to catch the shell as it was gracefully manuvered alongside the dock. Slow motion, performed quietly, is considered the "Tai Chi" of

---

[12] T. S. Eliot, *Four Quartets* (New York, NY: Harcourt, 1943).

rowing. It is the only method by which the athlete can self-analyze his movements accurately. In addition to using quiet sitting as part of the warm up and long steady state rows, it can be used as part of the warm down.

For Parmenides, the father of logic, the practice of quiet sitting or lying quietly was a cornerstone of his teaching 2500 years ago. I once thought that meditation and quiet sitting was only an Eastern practice, but here we have an early Greek practicing what he referred to as "incubation." Parmenides used this practice for healing, developing stillness and silence, and for enhancing man's internal spirit. Somehow, today's athlete has to find similar quiet spaces and moments in order to advance their skill. Muhammad Ali's championship preparation reinforces the importance of quiet, where he utilized the services of a non-English speaking Spanish masseur for his daily four hours of massage. He used this quiet time to regenerate and reset the physical body and to feel the recovery of his inner power. Ali's objective for quiet was very similar to Parmenides' "incubation" method for healing. It is a similar situation to what wounded animals do in the wild: they retreat to the woods, lie down and sleep.

So, this practice of quiet sitting serves the purpose of regenerating or resetting each athlete for the actual training session. With a few minutes of quiet sitting the athlete will be more focused for the practice. Rusty Callow, the great coach at the Naval Academy in the 1950s, would have his crew sit quietly for an hour before practice in order to restore balance to their bodies, especially the overtaxed central nervous system, after a long day of intensive classes and military drills. Fitzpatrick always insisted that the sculler sit quietly before doing a racing piece in order to review in his mind what was to follow. Taking a few quiet moments before the practice session probably insures a better effort. So, the coach should insist that the athletes take amoment to establish a focus before doing the piece.

In the late 19th century, Ned Hanlan, the great Canadian sculler, like Parmenides, was not saddled with the noise of the automobile and the busyness of the city on his quiet island home in Toronto harbor. He was therefore free to reflect, study and develop his inner self and his sculling skills. Hanlan on his quiet, solitary sojourns on Toronto Harbour was very studious of how his frail craft moved under all types of water and wind conditions. However, his inspiration for further improvement came from quietly observing an ordinary kitchen clock. "While watching it one day my attention was attracted by the steady swing of the pendulum. It swung backward and forward, but I could not detect, by closest observation, where the swing ended. That was my cue. I resolved to become a rowing pendulum." This is a distinct example of heightened awareness effecting skill development. Interestingly, Hanlan's new movement originated from his quiet reflections and materialized in the form of an effortless, subtle swing action. Hanlan discovered and utilized this unconscious, pendular movement of the trunk very effectively in his sculling over 100 years ago. The superb Russian sculler Ivanov displayed this same continuous, subtle trunk action in his sculling in the 1950s and 1960s (Ivanov's swing was more subtle because of his longer track bed compared to Hanlan's). However, for both athletes is was a clear case of integrating the subtle body swing with the run of the shell.

In rowing, to be effective, the athlete performs mentally centered in the physical space of a moving shell. When you row this way there is no past or future, there is only the present moment. This is a quality of mind that is necessary for effective racing. You come to view the race as a single stroke replicated. The Canadian coach Al Morrow speaks about this quality in his Olympic pair in 1992 - McBean and Heddle. "They maintained focus with only a half length lead on their competitors. They remained in the present moment, focusing on their own performance of the stroke cycle - an excellent example of stroke by stroke racing."[13]

Meditation continually expands our awareness. The athlete attempts to be aware of the body movements, thoughts and emotions. Eventually, these three aspects of awareness become one. During the meditation session the athlete makes no attempt to suppress the thoughts, he simply lets the thoughts come into the mind and lets them go out. As psychologist Charles Tart explains, "Ideas keep us living in an abstraction instead of the actual sensory reality."[14] We learn to quiet what the Buddhists refer to as the "Monkey Mind." It is a process of letting go of ideas and thoughts, and observing one's mind. This is a very beneficial skill at regattas when the coach and athlete are trying to maintain their relaxed focus amid all the activity. Eventually, the coach and

[13] Al Morrow, *Coaching* (presented at the The Joy of Sculling, Saratoga, NY, December 2000).

[14] Charles J. Tart, *Mind Science: Meditation Training for Practical People* (Novato, CA: Wisdom Editions, 2001).

athlete can develop their practice so that they can sit up to 10 to 20 minutes per session. Thich Nhat Hanh, a Vietnamese Buddhist monk has written extensively on this subject and writes, "Sitting meditation is very healing....sitting and breathing, we produce our true presence in the here and now and offer it to our community and to the world. This is the purpose of sitting, being here, fully alive, and fully present."[15] And, I would add, fully engaged.

[15] Thich Nhat Hanh, *Peace Is Every Step: The Path of Mindfulness in Everyday Life* (New York, NY: Bantam Books, 1991).

Visualization

Visualization is introduced early in the training through the use of simulation exercises for technique enhancement and later in the training cycle for race simulation (see Table 1.1). This type of training is used extensively in other sports such as boxing, downhill and nordic skiing, synchronized swimming, golf, baseball and track and field. It is similar to the boxer shadow boxing, the golfer taking practice swings, the synchronized swimmer performing her moves on land or the basketball player at the free throw line practicing the shot without the ball. Note how often do we see the golfer practice a swing at the tee before taking the actual shot, or the figure skater practicing the movements of her routine on land before the start of her performance.

The use of simulation exercises by Fitzpatrick established his genius and creativity. The exercises served as a "pump-primer" for visualization - aka "The Mind's Eye." These exercises develop the coach's and the athlete's awareness of the whole stroke. The simulation exercises also have the effect of slowing down the athlete's movements in order to perfect the skills. In the moment when visualization occurs, accuracy takes the priority over power. The simulation exercises provide a clearer picture of the movement for the young athlete, and are also an effective introduction to mental training.

During the off-water training in the winter, simulation exercises performed without the oar-handle break down the stroke into parts, with multiple repetitions performed on each of the parts. The drills can be done on the ergometer, or in the rowing tank or in a pool side trainer. These exercises

Table 2.2 Visualization	
Meditative Method on Land	• Rowing simulation exercises on land • Good posture sitting position • Use a small object and then recreate image of it in your head, repeat this until the image is clear in your mind
Meditative Method on Water	• Eyes closed rowing • Concentrate while staring at neck of person in front of you and visualizing bladework • Feathered Rowing for bodywork and bladework
Practice Schedule on Land	• Visualization 3x weekly at 10' per session lying down • Include concentration 1x week • Integral yoga for ~ 5-10' daily with breathing and posture focus • Group visualization, coxswains lead and call race.
Practice Schedule on Water	• 2' on, 1' off 5x a week, eyes closed/concentrated rowing respectively • 2-3' feathering rowing 3-4x weekly, as a warm-up and drill
Training Phase	• Throughout the whole year for technique • During pre-competition and competition phase

are usually done at the beginning of a training session for 10 to 15 minutes or for the total time during a technique-intensive training session. This type of drilling leads to improved individual coordination of movements and improved group timing.

These first three exercises are practiced without the arms involved. The arms remain relaxed at the sides, hanging freely as the trunk swings.

a. Sit at back of slide, legs fully extended, swing from hips beginning from beyond the perpendicular by 15/20° to slightly in front of the perpendicular towards the front stops - no slide.
b. Swing from or pivot from the hips beginning in front of the perpendicular to full reach of trunk - full slide - drift forward.
c. Swing from beyond perpendicular (20°) to full slide and full reach.

Athletes should execute the remaining exercises again without the oar handle but now simulating the arm actions. In this way, the athlete's imagination is getting a workout as well. It is important that the coach carefully monitor the hand placement and dynamic hand levels as the athlete moves up and down the slide, reinforcing the level shoulders and level hands.

d. Assume the position described in exercise No. 1 and simulate arm/hand action at finish - extend arms, no swing.
e. Combine exercises No. 1 and 4 - arm and swing action with no slide, emphasize flat wrists over knees
f. Assume the position described in exercise No. 2 - incorporate arms and move to full reach, emphasize hands raising from toes to full reach
g. Assume the position described in exercise No. 1 - combining swing and arms, total movements on the recovery

h. Leg drive from the balls of the feet - full slide. Feel the pressure move from the feet to the lower legs to the quadriceps.

i. Sit at the front end - move from hips and swing back to backstops, combine body

j. Sit at front stops - raise wrists, raise hands in a roll movement that mimics the inverse of the release action

k. Pull with arms, shoulders and leg drive from balls of feet - drive only

l. Full stroke

A variation of the simulation exercises includes aligning the ergometers side by side in order to develop the precision of the individual movements and the group timing. Then the coach guides the athletes "up and down" the slide bed indicating to the athletes where to stop at various points on the slide. The coach checks the accuracy of the seat positions on the slide, the hand levels, and the leg and trunk angles. Another drill for seat/slide position awareness is rowing part strokes including quarter slide front, half slide middle, quarter slide back, and three quarter slide. The quarter slide back end drill is particularly important because this part of the stroke is viewed as the whole cycle in minature. This particular drill is a study in subtlety, relaxation and good athletic movement. It is the basis for a relaxed recovery. All of these drills can be done with or without the handle.

This type of drilling ingrains the group timing. Eventually the drills evolve into slow motion rowing and mindfulness training. The programing of these simulation exercises requires creativity from the coach. These exercises, employed with the Yale

Lightweights in the late 1960s, created dramatic results during the winter tank work. The athletes displayed flawless bladework with marked precision and accuracy, tight body movements in the sense that there were no loose ends, and the individual segments of head, trunk, arms, and legs moved deliberately, disciplined and subtle. There was little or no wasted energy.

It came as a total shock to witness the extent of improvement in their timing after three weeks of concentrated drilling in the tanks. The effect carried through to the actual rowing and was almost immediately evident when training resumed on the water in the spring: the boat balance was exquisite. In the eight, the effect produced was almost like having one blade on the port side and one blade on the starboard side. Long rows by eight were immediately feasible, so the crews established an excellent aerobic base early in the spring season. Bob Fitzpatrick never prepared me for how well these drills would benefit the crew.

When off the water, the dominance of ubiquitous ergometer tests scores ignores the other uses for the ergometer, including endurance training, technique drills and the highly effective simulation exercises for timing of the body. We need to see the ergometer not only as a measuring tool, but also as a simulator for developing awareness, mindfulness, timing, coordination, accuracy, visualization skills and rhythm. In addition, the ergometer provides an opportunity to play and feel the relationship between economy of movement and power. On the ergometer, the athlete can also closely monitor the stillness evident in various parts of his body, a form of mindfulness. Thus, he learns to conserve his energy.

Another helpful exercise to learn conservation of motion is to direct the athletes to row poorly. Examples of poor rowing include: shooting the tail, breaking the arms early and opening the trunk early. The athletes quickly feel how difficult and laborious it is when rowing poorly. This is playing, and the athletes get to laugh at themselves: they have fun. When they return to the correct pattern, the rowing feels so much easier. Then they are more likely to understand and feel the conservation of energy.

The coach must serve as a conductor or choreographer during these visualization exercises, making corrections on hand, leg, trunk, and arm positions where necessary. This is especially true when coaching crews of multiple athletes where the stroke cycle image for visualization needs to be the same among all participants. The coach in this role develops deeper feeling for the various parts of the stroke cycle from his own understanding and demonstrations of the movements. These demonstrations, when done on a regular basis, strengthens the bond between the coach and his athletes. His body actions become a part of the athlete's reference and are a valuable resource for him. We see this type of activity with the hockey, tennis, baseball, basketball, track, and swim coaches where the coach is in the practice area. The rowing coach has this same opportunity, especially during the winter land workouts. Before the water workouts he can demonstrate some aspect of the stroke cycle and can do the same from his position in the coaching launch. However, to be an effective conductor or choreographer, the coach must become skillful in his demonstrations.

Drills can also use the body parts to simulate various aspects of the stroke cycle. For example, the coach simulates the blade action using his hands. Then the athletes follow this demonstration attempting the same movements using their hands. What I discovered at Yale was that the athletes were imitating their particular understanding of the entry action in the water with their hands. So if you wanted to modify their blade action it was helpful if you did this on land first using the hand simulations. The hand simulations can be an effective coaching tool to describe the entry and the release. A skilled simulation exercise with the hands is to have one hand describing the movement of the oar handle, and one hand describing the path of the blade. At the same time, with eyes closed, you visualize the patterns of both actions. This particular exercise demonstrates how the fingers can execute the entry and release actions with "flow." Any post-practice discussion with Fitzpatrick always entailed a great deal of hand motion to describe the bladework and body actions; it was always pure pleasure to watch his athletic hands/fingers describe the simple movements of the release and entry.

In addition to the hands, athletes can simulate both the trunk and leg movements of the stroke on the recovery and drive phases by placing one foot on a bench. Another body exercise is the group trunk swing with the crew straddling a bench in a sitting position. From the same position the arm action can be employed by first raising them to shoulder level in front of the body, then lowering the arms to the side of the body, an entry drill. the second drill with the arms for the release is pulling the extended arms/hands towards the sternum, into the release position and back out simulating the rowing action at the release, elbows in, elbows out. With this approach, the athletes internalize the movement pattern and eventually the trunk movement becomes well-timed and instinctive, a simple glide forward to the entry. The athletes improve their understanding of the pattern and their ability to duplicate this action on the water. The technique of the body and the movement of the oar handle become a part of his total being — mind, body, spirit.

A simulation drill on the water is feathering rowing. You keep the blade feathered, turning the edge of the blade opposite to the direction of the body movement in the shell. This prevents the blade from getting caught. At all times the blade is feathered. When the individual or the crew becomes more proficient, the blades can be balanced off the water. Simulation is an excellent form of cross-training and an excellent recovery activity on lighter load days.

As mentioned above, it is important that the athletes have a clear and uniform picture of the stroke cycle. I recall being present when Jack Nicholson of Canada asked his World Championship quad to write a description of the action of the recovery. Each of the four athletes wrote different versions. I thought to myself how much better they would have performed if they had a uniform perspective on and approach to the recovery in their minds. This exercise is an excellent way to verify the athlete's perspective and understanding of specific movements in the cycle.

The team can also try to visualize some aspect of the stroke cycle from either a sitting position on the floor, in the boat, or on the ergometer. This again is an excellent device to advance the athlete's technique. This represents a variation of quiet sitting. Visualization on land requires a quiet place and a good sitting position and a two or three dimensional small object placed in front of you (i.e. your watch). At home, a candle in a darkened room is a good prop. After concentrating on the object for a few minutes, close your eyes and try to envision a mental reproduction of the object in your mind. If any part of the object is not sufficiently clear, open your eyes and correct your observation and memory until the image coincides with the original object.

Dwight Stones, the bronze medalist high jumper in the 1976 Olympics, spoke of this practice - "I see a translucent image of myself coming out of myself. I watch to see if I will make it. Many times I don't. I have to concentrate harder."

To create uniformity in the movements of the stroke, the final on water visualization practice is to have each rower concentrate on the movements of the crew member immediately in front of them and behind them. In the latter case, you are expecting the person to image his movements with the person behind him. Ideally, the stroke person attempts to visualize the bow person and vice versa. This imaging is also a way for the athlete to connect with the rhythm and energy of the person in front of him, or even two seats in front, as well as anyone rowing behind him. It goes a long way to creating a uniform pattern in the crew. This practice is usually inserted into a steady state row by a simple directive from the coach or coxswain. Another effective drill for developing awareness and connection, is to have the crews row parallel and try to be perfectly synchronized by seats; each member of the crew has to watch the seat in the opposite crew,concentrating on his own rowing and the pattern of the person opposite him. This a very productive way to end practice

The imaging must be reinforced with the coach's choreography, demonstrations and video, so that the mental picture is clear and precise for the athletes. Again, an accurate image of the stroke cycle must become part of them. This is an example of Fitzpatrick's Mind's Eye.

Visualization can also be race-related, incorporating mindfulness and concentration. In the later stages of the training cycle, short pieces (500 meters, 1000 meters, etc.) can be quickly visualized in the boat during training sessions, so that each piece has a focus, such as stroke rate, rhythm, shell run, or the race plan. As the rowing season progresses, the total race simulation is introduced and practiced as a visualization method. This can be done on land with the coxswain leading the race visualization session or on the water doing a complete race simulation. For example, J. Kenneth Doherty, a former long-time track coach at the University of Pennsylvania, wrote, "An excellent method of 'mental training' a few days before a competition is to cover the exact distance of one's race at a slower pace during which one concentrates on simulating the race itself. In so doing, play the role of how you feel as well as what you do."[16] For the 2001 Tour de France, simulating the race route was a major part of Lance Armstrong's preparation.

The complete race day simulation involves every feature of the race day, including weigh-ins (for

---

[16] Jimmy Joy, *The Art of Sculling* (presented at NAAO (Now US Rowing) Annual Meeting, Syracuse, NY, December 8 1978).

lightweights), the meal times, the race plan, the warm-up and warm-down activity, not just the execution of the race itself. This should be simulated at least two or three times before arriving at the regatta site, and usually on days when you have a 2000m time trial scheduled. The athletes arrive at the regatta site well-prepared. They "take ownership" of the "regatta site" by walking around and absorbing all the activity without being distracted or intimidated. In the pre-race practice on the course, they also are instructed to look out of the boat to familiarize themselves with the important landmarks. All of these measures make them feel comfortable - relaxed and focused and aware of their surroundings.

In a complete race day simulation, the coach lets the athletes determine their schedule - eating, concentration and visualization practices, workouts, warm-ups and helps them develop a simple race plan. This plan should include considering the 2000 meters a true sprint with an elevated stroke rate. The other components of the plan should include maintaining good quality of movement and length for each stroke, and a simple goal of racing the second half of the race harder than the first half. The athletes should then feel that they have done their homework, and are well prepared mentally, physically, nutritionally, technically and emotionally when race day arrives. Their integrity is intact because they have completed their training, and so they have the confidence that their training has put them in a position to compete for the championship. In large part, this orginates from the development of a powerful, internal, quiet and visual mind.

Another effective drill for racing scheduled during the competitive season, is the 'hard and harder" piece. Every piece is rowed, first half hard, and second half harder. So a 500 meter piece would be rowed, 250 meter hard, followed by a second 250 meter harder. All pieces are segmented into "hard and harder" during this phase of the training. The athlete tries to visualize and feel the difference internally. The coach can bring this "hard and harder" down to a single stroke sequence with the first half of the drive hard and the second half of the drive harder followed by an easy stroke. The intent is to instill into the athlete the mental framework of racing the second half of the race harder than the first half.

Additionally, the athletes can practice the first four or five strokes of the start at low intensity every time they stop and resume their rowing. This is something that Fitzpatrick insisted should occur every time the sculler stopped rowing and then restarted. It is unfathomable why coaches would have their crews resume rowing from the release position rather than from the entry, a missed opportunity to ingrain the pattern of the start without incurring lactate buildup. Phil Jackson puts another twist on visualization as he explains,

> *"Visualization is an important tool for me. Coaching requires a free-ranging imagination, but during the heat of the moment it is easy to get so tightly wound up that you strangle on your own creativity. Visualization is the bridge I use to link the grand vision of the team I conjure up every summer to the evolving reality on the court. That vision becomes a working sketch that I adjust, refine, and sometimes scrap altogether as the season develops...Before each game I usually*

*do forty five minutes of Visualization at home
to prepare my mind and to come up with last
minute adjustments."[17]*

According to the legendary Aikido master
Morihei Uesiba, "The opponent is within...Training is
not for correcting others; it is for correcting your own
mind."[18] Phil Jackson, in his mental game
preparation, practices the philosophy of Uesiba. The
simulation/visualization exercises are low technology
but have high value for the athlete and the coach. For
the rowing coach, he can also review his daily
practice schedule and practice venue, visualize it and
be well prepared. For the student, this skill is easily
transferred to the classroom when she has to make a
presentation.

Teilhard De Chardin in his book, *The
Phenomenon of Man,*"recognized the existence of a
conscious inner face that everywhere duplicates the
material, external face which alone is considered by
science."[19] Indeed, visualization takes us deep into
our internal face. It assist the athlete in being more
athletic, organic and fluid rather than moving in a
mechanistic fashion. With all of these various
simulation practices, the athlete's mind increases his
mental plasticity. This has has serious implications
for his rowing and for life applications outside the
shell.

---

[17] Jackson, *Sacred Hoops: Spiritual Lessons of a Hardwood Warrior.*

[18] Richard Strozzi Heckler, *In Search of the Warrior Spirit: Teaching
Awareness Disciplines to the Green Berets* (Berkeley, CA: North
Atlantic Books, 2003).

[19] Pierre Teilhard de Chardin, *The Phenomenon of Man* (New York, NY:
Harper, 1959).

Relaxation

The third practice is relaxation.* As a coach, introduce relaxation early in the preparation phase for technique learning, and again during the competitive phase for releasing any tension at regattas and developing the ability to race effortlessly. On-water methods for relaxation include slow motion rowing, part stroke rowing, the emphasis is a relaxed grip for rowing and sculling, "easy speeds", and rowing at 90% effort. The "90 percent law" is a practice that was widely employed by former Olympic coach Bud Winter's track athletes as a stimulant for relaxation, faster movement, more strength, and less fatique, and greater sense of well being.[20] Initially, coaches might find their crews rowing faster at 90% than at the 100% effort, due to the excessive motion and check created by crews trying to row too hard at 100%. However, coaches should ultimately see very little difference in appearance between the 90% and 100% pressures if the athlete rows relaxed. So, what is a good drill for this? An excellent practice on the ergometer is three twenty-minute pieces with three minutes passive rest between the pieces. The athlete discovers that his times are not that far above his best 20 minutes times. The athlete observes that a consistent level of relaxed, endurance intensity is achieveable.

---

* Note: Relaxation can, however, be inserted into the technical training for novices early in their learning stage. It assists in the learning process by eliminating tension, which inhibits developing a feeling for the stroke.

[20] Al Chung-liang Huang and Jerry Lynch, *Thinking Body, Dancing Mind: Taosports for Extraordinary Performance in Athletics, Business and Life* (New York, NY: Bantam Books, 1994).

Table 2.3 Relaxation	
Meditative Method on Land	• Progressive relaxation techniques • Tensing and relaxing specific body parts while lying on your back
Meditative Method on Water	• Alternate a number of strokes with a tensing of the body followed by relaxing the body for a similar number of strokes • Rowing at 90% effort • Easy speeds, gradually building up the rating and intensity over 30 strokes
Practice Schedule on Land	• Relaxation 3 times a week at 5-10' per session • Continue quiet sitting 2 times a week at 3-10' per session • Yoga ~ 5-15' Daily
Practice Schedule on Water	• Row 10 strokes tense, 10 strokes relaxed • Row at 90% 2x weekly • Easy speeds, 30 strokes 3x weekly or 4 to 5 sets at 2x weekly • 3x weekly quiet rowing while checking posture and alignment
Training Phase	• Second month of preparatory phase • During competitive phase

To begin the relaxation training, emphasize the relaxed hand hold of the oar handle. This is especially helpful for the novice who too often squeeze the handle so that the energy goes into it, instead of holding it lightly. If you pull with the fingers hooked around the handle and a relaxed hand hold, the energy goes through the handle and the drive is linear. Encourage sweep rowers to use a two-handed release, the "roll release," and feather with flat wrists or a minimum of wrist action for extracting the blade from the water and moving into the recovery. Thus, the athlete creates a stroke without a "division of labor" for the hands' actions. This approach relaxes the forearms and shoulder girdle. It is probably the most important skill the novice should master before moving on to other aspects of the stroke.

The release was the starting point for Fitzpatrick for teaching technique, and his rowers practiced it until they had mastered the movement. Later, as the athlete progresses, long steady rows at low rate emphasizing the light hand hold and flat wrists at the release are incorporated into the training. The goal is to have the oar handle and oar become a part of the athlete, a natural extension of his hands and arms.

To aid in developing a relaxed feeling, have the athletes perform a set number of strokes in complete body tension, "tighten up," followed by the same number of strokes as completely relaxed as possible. The athlete is encouraged to feel the difference, especially, the anticipated increase in shell run, and the longer stroke length during the relaxation strokes. I have witnessed this drill done effectively with both elite and high school crews.

Coaches can also employ the "easy speed" drill where the crew moves the rate of striking from 32 to 40 with ease. They must stay relaxed as the power and rate increase over short pieces of 20 to 30 strokes. This drill was introduced in July of 2008 to the Canadian women's lightweight double, Tracey Cameron and Melanie Kok and they took to it immediately. They also liked the catchy terminology for the drill, "easy speed." Previously they were straining to scull higher than their base rating. With an "easy speed" approach, their sculling flowed. Coach Al Morrow reported after the games that they carried this idea and practice all the way to their bronze medal performance at the Beijing Olympics. This drill can be used in the warm up, warm down or as a separate workout.

The idea for this drill came from my own running. You slowly and steadily increase your stride until you are sprinting. Building up the speed in this fashion is based on rowing at "90%" physical effort, which parallels Fitzpatrick's philosophy of "pull what you can handle." On water, Fitz's philosophy prevents the blade from washing out or bouncing through the drive; the blade remains at blade depth. So, the 90% law and "pull what you can handle" are excellent methods for establishing the flow and rhythm in the stroke cycle, an obviously crucial component to boat speed during racing and training. The two concepts are also extremely effective during the winter ergometer workouts, as a real challenge presents itself for the athlete to feel the body rhythm without the benefit of shell run.

Another drill for the winter months to assist in the development of relaxation and rhythm is the repeated ¼ front, followed by a full drive, then ¼ back, followed by a full recovery — a four part drill. This is an excellent, enjoyable and relaxed drill for improving the feel for shell run and rhythm on the water, once the timing and rhythm are established indoors.

Richard Burnell in his book, *The Oxford Pocket Book of Sculling Training*, wrote, "Rhythm is sculling in harmony with the movement of the shell."[21] In a

---

[21] Richard Burnell, *The Oxford Pocket Book of Sculling Training* (London: Oxford University Press, 1962).

complimentary statement Sugar Ray Robinson[*], the greatest boxer of all time, believed that "rhythm is everything in boxing. Every move you make starts with your heart, and that's in rhythm or you're in trouble."[22] It seems that Sugar Ray went deep into himself in order to feel the rhythm. The use of the jump rope by the boxer is a good warmup and an effective exercise for fostering the athlete's rhythmic endurance. In my coaching, this exercise was used extensively, especially during the winter training. Jumping rope fosters athleticism. So for this reason, training for rhythm through jumping rope is a practice that individuals and crews should have the experience of mastering. Rhythm requires that the athlete to be more in touch with their body and the shell.

During the winter months relaxation sessions are usually done in the supine position on land with the eyes opened or closed for 5 to 15 minutes at the end of practice. The coach conducts this process, which involves a systematic tensing and relaxing of various parts of the body. The coach moves the focus through your body parts from toes to head, up and down each side of the body and continue with the major segments of the body: the arms, the legs and ultimately the whole body tenses and relaxes. Finally, the coach provides the athletes a few minutes of total relaxation with the eyes closed and the lights off. This last phase is a totally refreshing and restorative moment for the athletes. Relaxation practice is usually done one or two times weekly. For students,

---

[*] See Sugar Ray Robinson in Notes & Suggested Readings Chapter

[22] Sugar Ray Robinson and Dave Anderson, *Sugar Ray: The Sugar Ray Robinson Story* (New York, NY: Viking Press, 1970).

this is a very effective tension reliever during examination periods. The body is reset at the end of practice with this relaxation exercise and the student is now ready for an evening of study.

In addition to rhythm, the other quality that helps immensely with relaxation is humor. Ken Wilber expressed the importance of the trait when he wrote the following:

> "Transcendence restores humor. Spirit brings smiling. Suddenly, laughter returns. Too many representatives of too many movements - even very good movements, such as feminism, ecology, and spiritual studies - seem to lack humor altogether. In other words they lack lightness, they lack a distance from themselves, a distance from ego and its grim game of forcing others to conform to its contours. There is a self-transcending humor or there is the game of egoic power... No wonder H.L.Mencken wrote that 'Every third American devotes himself to improving and lifting up his fellow citizens, usually by force; this messianic delusion is our national disease.' Perhaps we should all trade two pounds of ego for one ounce of laughter."[23]

Wilber emphasizes humor and laughter as important qualities for the development of relaxation for both individuals and the team. What immediately comes to mind upon reading this quote is the extremely earnest humorless Bolshevik commissar, Pasha, in Dr. Zhivago, or some overly serious and zealous

---

[23] Ken Wilber, *One Taste: The Journals of Ken Wilber* (Boston, MA: Shambhala, 1999).

coach who is one-dimensional in life and in sport. Dick Vermeil is a prime example of this type in professional athletics. The end of his tenure with the Philadelphia Eagles demonstrated how constant yelling and fear drove the team to failure on almost all fronts. There was no humor or spirit to his style. Both the overly dedicated Communist commissar and the extremely work-alcoholic coach are idealogues viewing life through a narrow and serious prism.

However, great crews that readily come to mind that had this quality of humor were the American 1964 gold medal eight and the Canadian 1984 gold medal eight. Both coaches, Rosenberg and Campbell, provided the necessary space for the athletes to enjoy the total experience. This is a powerful quality that is found in effective athletes and teams. Humor is a quality that I witnessed in the Hobart and William Smith crews in the 1990s. At the time, a coach inquired how this spirit was developed and I felt that both my humor and the athletes' personal empowerment were the key ingredients. I recall that the athletes and coaches laughed a great deal. Also, it helped to have the correct balance in the training program between work, rest, and recovery. It is conjecture, but humor and spirit may be worth a half length on the water.

As race day approaches, it is critical and crucial that the tapering and peaking phases are carefully planned to refine the development of the body and mind by integrating the mental, physical, and technical traning (see Table 2.6 later in this chapter). This planning helps in keeping the situation relaxed and focused. There are three goals for racing well:

a. Improve the mental focus
b. Develop more relaxed, fluid body movements
c. Improve the run of the shell

The coach orchestrates the situation so that internal anxieties, frustration, anger and fear are minimized. Neil Campbell never made a negative comment to the crew for the last two months prior to the 1984 Olympic final.[24] Consequently, the crew and coach were confident, spirited, determined and relaxed. This approach also enhances the flow of the body movements and increases the outward power and energy by the efficient use of power. The athletes were ready for racing. This illustrates the relationships between relaxation and the flow of the body. The smooth, effortless action of the body represents the refined inner consciousness of the athlete's mind. Relaxation and *flow* are inextricably linked. This philosophy of an integrated program emphasizes the ultimate objective of a mental training program — the experiencing of *flow*.

---

[24] Neil Campbell, 1984. *Discussion of Canadian M8+ Training for the 1984 Los Angeles Olympics.*

Concentration

Concentration is probably the most difficult practice and requires a lot of patience and perseverance. Concentration is a contraction of our focus — towards "one pointedness" of the mind. Again in the winter months and for the experienced rower, this exercise is initiated by sitting on the floor with good posture. It allows us to slow down, encounter stillness and silence, and to focus and relax. There are three methods that can be used on land to develop the athlete's powers of concentration:

a. Focusing on an object.
b. Counting breaths.
c. Doing a set routine of concentrative yoga stretching.

In the first case, the athlete takes up a sitting position on the floor with good posture. A small object is placed about 18 inches in front of the participant. The eyes are open and remain focused on the object for one to three minutes. The athlete must avoid any deviation of thought and focus during this period.

To use the counting breaths method, the athlete assumes a good sitting position with eyes either open or closed. The counted breaths are to be full and deep with the breathing originating from the abdomen. He breathes in for a six count and breathes out for a six count, making it rhythmic. Breathe through the nose and try to fill the body to a maximum before emptying the lungs as much as possible. When you inhale, you will depress the chest, distend the abdomen (large protruding belly)

Table 2.4 Concentration	
Meditative Method on Land	• Check for good posture • Two Methods • Breath counting using abdominal/nasal breathing • Concentrate on a small object placed in front of you • Try to let go of thoughts • Stay present with no-mind, larger self, no boundaries • Complete person-body, mind, spirit (flow and integration)
Meditative Method on Water	• Intensive drills — entry, drive, release, recovery • Technique days • Easy speeds • Fartleks
Practice Schedule on Land	• Concentration 3x weekly for 8' per session • Relaxation 1x weekly for 10' • Quiet sitting 2x weekly • Integral Yoga 5-15' daily for breathing, concentration, posture
Practice Schedule on Water	• 10-60' 3x weekly • Incorporate relaxation at start of drills • Count number of strokes you can hold one thought • 1' highs closely monitoring stroke quality • Concentrate on each stroke for set pieces • Easy speeds 3x weekly, 30 strokes & 3-4 pieces • Fartlek 1x weekly • 10,10,10,10 at light, firm, hard, and quick x 10 • Slow motion rowing 4x weekly
Training Phase	• Pre-competition phase • Competitive phase

and push the diaphragm down. As you exhale, you distend and raise the chest, pull the abdomen in and raise the diaphragm. Each breath must be slow and complete. Count the breaths by ten up to sixty for ten minutes. Remember to check your sitting position.

The third method for concentration is integral yoga stretching which the athletes can do as a team. A routine of four to five exercises should be led by a team member who is proficient in the movements. Each position or side is held for a six breath count, and four to six repetitions are performed before moving quickly to the next exercise in the routine. All the exercises are performed from the floor or a combination of the floor and standing positions. This practice is referred to as integral yoga since it combines the meditation, the posture/exercises, and the breathing. Yoga is an excellent practice for warm-up or warm-down and the total time can be 10 to 15 minutes. The group can perform the various exercises together for timing, led by the captain, or a yoga proficient athlete.

The athlete needs to consciously control all mental effort while concentrating. The mental focus narrows and the mind becomes "one point", as shown in Leonard Perlmutter's chart (Figure 2.1) on the following page. In the shell, this one-pointedness expresses itself when the athlete concentrates his focus on the nape of the neck of the person immediaterly in front of him, or by looking over the stern from the stroke or sculling seat. Elite and junior crews can achieve this singular focus as witnessed by Columbia Women's Head Coach, Melanie Onufrieff: "It was an impressive display of *one pointed attention* observing Coach Elizabeth Corman's* 15 and 16 year old athletes from the

---

* Elizabeth Corman was a rower at William Smith College where the program being discussed in this book was employed.

Seattle Lakeside school doing their daily concentration exercises."[25]

Figure 2.1 Pointed and Dissipated Attention

Dissipated Attention:

An undisciplined mind randomly misdirects potentially creative energy

Past   Future

One-Pointed Attention:

A focused mind directs its energy to a single point and experiences pleasure, clarity and creativity.

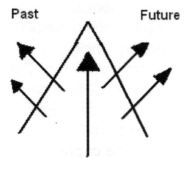

Leonard Perlmutter '07

I recall seeing the video of the women's single sculls final in the 1999 World Championships where Ekaterina Karsten remained focued on her shell for the entire race by looking just beyond the stern of her shell. Only occasionally did her eyes shift, using her peripheral vision to view the field of scullers on her right. So, for the most part, the focus is narrowed to the immediate environment inside the boat. This could include practice pieces where you hold a particular focus (bladework, timing, etc.) for a number of strokes or a set time.

The use of coaching intensive "technique days" is another cxcellent method for improving the

---

[25] Personal Correspondence, 2007.

athlete's and coach's concentration. The intent is to improve the body movements and shell run. The method is quite simple. Select a quiet stretch of water about 1,500 to 2,000 meters long. Do multiple sets of drills on various parts of the stroke cycle for about 90 minutes. The coach monitors the quality of the performance very closely, frequently stopping and checking the movements of the crew. It is important that the crew realizes that the individual movements must be executed as accurately as possible. The shortened stretch of rowing intensifies the athlete's focus and the frequent turning around provides a welcome pause from that intense concentration. Use this practice one or two times in the preparation phase and two or three times in the pre-competition phase where the emphasis shifts from "training to train" to "training to compete, and "training to win."[26]

Towards the end of the training year large gains are realized by fine-tuning the movements, and this improves the mental focus. During the final stages of on-water training, practices use whole movements where the objective is to integrate the body action with the oars and the shell run. Again, the concentration must focus on each stroke.

The primary benefit of practicing for smooth movement is the development of concentration and the merging of action and awareness that is made possible by centering the mind on a limited stimulus field. To insure that people will concentrate on their own actions, potentially intruding stimuli must be reduced or eliminated from our attention; this involves narrowing the consciousness. Geoffrey Page,

[26] Ted Daigenault, 1980s. *Terms from Training Plans Used with the Canadian National Team.*

a British rowing coach, wrote in 1963: "Rowing is a sport requiring intense and sustained concentration. Unless a crew can train itself to keep its mind on the job the clearance will diminish and the blade work will get 'woolly' towards the end of any stretch of work. The crew must learn to think for itself and to judge the pace of the boat; the crew must not rely on the coach to do it for them."[27]

During the training year, sometimes a concentration drill is scheduled at the end of practice, when the body is fatigued and the athlete must learn to hang on mentally. This brings to mind a wrestling drill that Coach Mike Yuhasz employed in preparing for championships. His best and most experienced wrestlers would be prepared by having them wrestle a fresh opponent every three minutes for a total of fifteen minuters. Rightly so, this drill was referred to as the "Killer Drill." The athlete had to maintain his focus and persevere even as he became more fatigued. The lessons learned from the "Killer Drill" have remained with me throughout my lifetime. The same lessons parallel those of finding enough energy to finish the last five hundred meter of a race. I often have contemplated how this drill could be incorporated into the preparation of a crew or sculler.

Quiet sitting for concentration also provides another opportunity for coaches to relate/participate with their athletes. It provides the coach balance, humanness, and a qualitative ingredient to the sport that has become distorted by excessive emphasis on competition and quantitative data. Concentration practice done on a regularly basis assists the coach

---

[27] Geoffrey Page, *Coaching for Rowing* (London, UK: Museum Press, 1963).

and the athlete in stepping outside their daily fast-paced culture to encounter learning from the stillness of the mind. We move from the quantitative and busy, to the qualitative and the essential. We realize how routine and "embedded" our lives are. In being self-aware, we become more spontaneous, more creative, and our minds, bodies, and spirits regenerate. We also experience a significant shift in our minds from the purely thinking or rational mode to a clearer intuitive mode.

In sport, decisions must be made quickly from moment to moment and a highly developed intuition is a very beneficial skill. Eventually the performance of any physical skill must evolve to this automatic or non-thinking stage in order to be most effective. The execution of the stroke cycle reflects this non-thinking by being totally reflexive and spontaneous. Also, we improve our level of patience and our ability to remain focused in the present moment. Our minds shift from linear to spatial time as we begin to achieve the automatic phase of training. The athlete simply knows what to do without thinking. The athlete's fully developed intuition may well be one of the primary goals of all training.

Mindfulness

The final meditative practice, mindfulness, is introduced into the training. Mindfulness, or awareness training, represents a high level form of meditation. It is the practice of "knowing what you are doing, while you are doing it, no matter what it may be."[28] Mindfulness enhances your ability to concentrate. Mindfulness must be reinforced on the water, in the weight room, on the ergometer and during any cross-training activity. Neil Campbell would not let his athletes have earphones during training because he felt it would interfere with their mind, body and spirit's connection. For this reason, television or music serve as unnecessary distractions when you are trying to connect the inner self with the body movements and with your environment. In a quiet setting the athlete learns to feel both his external and the deeper internal sources of his power.

In the spring of 2002 when Kobe Bryant and Phil Jackson were asked what contributed most to the championship play of the Los Angeles Lakers, they responded, "We were able to stay in the moment." Recently figure skater Brian Boitano, when asked what was the major contributing factor in his Olympic victory in 1988 responded, "I was able to stay in the present moment."[29] Parmenides referred to the elimination of distraction as the "Reality of the Now" — past or future do not enter into our thinking as we are fully centered in the present.

---

[28] Duane Elgin, *Awakening Earth: Exploring the Evolution of Human Culture and Consciousness* (New York, NY: Morrow, 1993).

[29] Readings from newspaper accounts of the competition

Table 2.5 Mindfulness	
Meditative Method on Land	• Body scanning, a progressive sensitivity technique with no judgment, just kinesthetic awareness • In the present you should have full awareness
Meditative Method on Water	• Slow motion rowing: check it • ¼ slow motion rowing from the back end, a miniature whole stroke
Practice Schedule on Land	• Mindfulness 3x weekly at 2-15' per session • Quiet sitting 1x weekly at 3-8' per session • Relaxation 3x weekly at 10' per session • Yoga ~ 5-15' daily • Simulation exercises
Practice Schedule on Water	• Slow motion rowing 5x weekly, as part of warm-up and warm-down • ¼ slide slow motion rowing 3x weekly for total awareness
Training Phase	• During preparatory phase • Remind athletes to be mindful throughout the year in all training environments: water, gym, erg, etc.

Some contemporary athletes such as Wayne Gretzky and Michael Jordan exemplified this skill to a high degree. They were totally aware of everyone on the ice or the court and where the puck or ball was at any given moment. This type of awareness training begins with consciousness of your body and then works outward to include the athlete's total environment. Awareness always precedes control.

In the winter, the primary technique for this practice is the body scan.[30] It is done from either a sitting or lying position with the eyes closed. Again, the coach leads the group. The athletes take a few moments to relax before the coach begins his directions. During the progressive scanning of the body parts, the athlete makes no judgment; they feel the targeted area and make a mental note of any pleasant, unpleasant or neutral sensations. Progressively, the coach asks the athletes to focus their attention on the right foot, lower leg, upper leg, abdomen, chest, shoulder, upper arm, lower arm, hand, neck, face, and head before moving to the left side and repeating the exercise in reverse order. Following these steps, the coach enlarges the focus to include both upper legs, both lower legs, both hands, both lower arms and finally both upper arms and add listening as the focus for the senses. Slowly open the eyes while continuing to listen and to sense. Look actively at things for a few seconds. At this point, your whole body is totally involved and integrated with the immediate environment. This whole procedure should be repeated for a total of two to fifteen minutes. This practice is scheduled during the later stages of the preparation phase and again during the pre-competition phase in order to reinforce this skill. However, coaches should constantly remind themselves that mindfulness should always be present in every aspect of a workout.

Additional mindfulness practice involves watching thoughts. The athletes should assume a

---

[30] Wes Nisker, *Buddha's Nature: Evolution as a Practical Guide to Enlightenment* (New York, NY: Bantam Books, 1998).

sitting position with good posture. The eyes remain open or partially closed. The meditator attempts to develop an impersonal attitude towards thoughts. He notes that the thought of this, or the desire for that, passes before the mind, and then passes from the mind, or is held by the mind. The present moment has our full attention, with no thoughts of the past or the future. Try to sit for three to eight minutes, increasing the time with ability. Again, employ this practice in both the pre-competition and competitive phases. Encourage the athletes to work in silence, whether in the shell, on the ergometer, or in the weight room.

Slow motion rowing represents one of the best ways to develop mindfulness on the water. In slowing down, the athlete becomes more aware of the individual movements, and he performs the skill with more accuracy and control. At the other end of the stroke rating spectrum is the hard twenty stroke pieces performed at forty strokes per minute. The goal is to complete twenty perfect strokes in thirty seconds. During this intense piece, the sculler is expected to monitor the quality of each stroke. I recall vividly the number of poor and rushed strokes in trying to reach a forty strokes per minute pace in the beginning of the season. During one of these pieces, I recall hitting the steel plated bulkhead at one corner of the finish line in St. Catharines; clearly a case of too much concentration and too little mindfulness. Somehow, the shell and myself stayed connected and in one piece.

As the season progressed however, the skills along with the patient consciousness evolved, and the strokes became flawless, fluid, and without rush. At the release the wrist action became minimal, the entries were cleaner and the overall bladework more precise. The concentration and mindfulness had evolved to new levels of proficiency. This is an excellent practice for raising the stroke rate while maintaining the length and quality of the stroke.

Duane Elgin states the need for balance between concentration and mindfulness:

> *"In cultivating our capacity to live more consciously, it is important to develop two qualities of conscious attention that balance one another - concentration and mindfulness. Concentration is the ability to focus on the precise center of our unfolding experience. Mindfulness is the ability to be aware of the panoramic totality of life...With a dynamic balance, each acts as a corrective against the excesses of the other. Nothing is left out of our experience, as both the details and the spacious context of our lives are embraced in our consciousness."[31]*

This quote captures the essence of Bob Fitzpatrick's teaching: the balance between mind, body and spirit, between the narrow situation and the expansive one, between the rational and the intuitional, between science and the experiential, between the meditative modes of concentration and mindfulness and between sport and life.

At this point, the communication between the coach and athlete and among the athletes does not have to be verbal. You simply know, anticipate and intuit the action around you. This highly developed

---

[31] Elgin, *Awakening Earth: Exploring the Evolution of Human Culture and Consciousness*.

state of personal mindfulness is the common thread between all of the various training methods used by the team. Slowing down, quiet sitting, experiencing stillness, relaxation drills and visualization sessions that include the simulation drills involve qualitative effort and movement. The concentration and mindfulness practice sessions with the entire team enhance the concentrative mindset. It should be noted that, as the athlete gained more experience, Fitzpatrick asked the athlete for more input as to what was happening on the water. So this reminds me of the story of quarterback Joe Montana coming off the field and the legendary coach of the San Francisco 49ers, Bill Walsh commented, "It must be hell out there Joe." Joe quickly turned to Walsh and said, "How the hell would you know?"[32]

If the coach has done his job properly, the athlete becomes a source of information that he must utilize in order to obtain more exact information. As a young high school football coach I remember giving full responsibilty to the quarterback to extract the team from a "deep hole" near our goaline. He did. This was a result of his being in the situation on the field and having a feel for what needed to happen. Rowing coaches can also look to well trained athletes for more exact information on what is happening in the shell.

Once the mental training skills are honed and the physical skills have reached the automatic stage, the athlete is now ready for racing. Table 2.6 provides an example of an integrated plan for the final stages of training.

---

[32] Readings from newspaper accounts of the competition

Integrating the Five Processes

Once the mental training skills are honed and the physical skills have reached the automatic stage, the athlete is now ready for racing. The figure below represents an annual view of a training plan that incorporates the five meditative processes.

Figure 2.2 Annual Periodization of Training

Competition Whole

Quiet Sitting - Flow

Seat/Blade Timing*

August

Preparatory I - Whole

Concentration

Posture & Bladework

Visualization (Race)

Visualization (Technique)

Relaxation

May

November

Bladework Concentration*

Relaxation - On Water

Pre-competition: Parts - Drills

Bodywork/Timing*

Preparatory II - Parts/Drills

Mindfulness

January

Mindfulness

* Note the Periodization of General Technique Training

Table 2.6 on the folowing page provides an example of an integrated plan for the final stages of training. Note that coach must diligently use the mental training to develop the "Mind's Eye" throughout the year to achieve the maximum benefit of the integrated approach.

Day	Physical Training	Mental Training	Technique
	Table 2.6 Integrated Program for Tapering and Peaking		
1	2x10' (long rest) or 3'-2'-1' with 5' rest @ 28, 30, 34 SPM	Day	Slow Motion
2	8-10x2' (regular rest) or Technique Day+	Quiet Sitting	Pull Throughs and Set-ins
3	2x1000m (long rest)	Visualization (before practice)	Feathering Rowing
4	4-5x1' (5' rest between pieces)	Relaxation (after practice)	¼ slide back end - quickly
5	45-50' steady state easy @ 18-22SPM	Concentration (after practice)	Slow Motion
6	1x2000m @ race rate	Visualization (pre) Relaxation (post)	Eyes Closed Rowing
7	Off or Easy Technique Work	Quiet Sitting	Intense Technique - 60'
8	3x5' or 2x8' long rest or "3x500m"+2x1000m"	Mindfulness (post-practice)	¼ Slide Front
9	4x1 (5' Rest Between Pieces)	Relaxation (after practice)	30 Stroke Easy Speeds
10	30' Easy + Starts or Fartlek 3', 2', 1', 30" x 2 @ slow, light, hard, quick	Concentration (after practice)	Pull Throughs and Set-ins from ¾ Slide
11	30' Easy + Starts	Relaxation (after practice)	¾ Slide with Trunk
12	30' Easy + Starts	Relaxation (after practice)	Slow Motion and Feathering Rowing
13	Big Race	Visualization(Pre-race) Relaxation (Inter-race)	¼ and ½ Slide Rowing during Warm Up
14	Big Race	Same as Day 13	Regeneration, Intensity, Rest, Efficiency

Integral Coaching

"Can we talk about the wholeness of life? Can one be aware of that wholeness if the mind is fragmented? You can't be aware of the whole if you are only looking through a small hole."

J. Krishnamurti

Integral means comprehensive, inclusive, and unified. It includes all of the parts that make up the whole. Outstanding coaches personify this mindset and live their philosophy. Their being and doing, their thinking and action are one. The coach attempts to integrate mind, matter and spirit. Volker Nolte of the University of Western Ontario is an excellent example as he integrates his teaching, coaching, research writing and family life. In many ways he reminds me of the young coach, Michael Yuhasz, when he was engaged in similar tasks at University of Western Ontario in the 1950s. The integral coaches like Nolte and Yuhasz are following the tradition of the early philosophers from antiquity such as Parmenides, who were healers and tutors, not abstract thinkers. They lived their philosophies. In understanding the athlete, the coach reaches an understanding of his own self. Percy Cerutty, Steve Fairbairn, and Phil Jackson are a few examples of this type of coach with Jackson and Cerutty including a significant internal dimension to the athlete's training. The outstanding historical example of integral coaching on this continent was the team coaching between the Pococks, George and Stan, at Lake washington and Frank Read at the University of British Columbia in the the 1950s and 1960s. The result was five Olympic medals, two gold and two silver, in the 1956 and 1960 Olympics. George visited Frank every month. According to one UBC oarsman, "all hell broke loose" after George left because of George's insightful criticisms. Also, Read, being independently wealthy, was able to bring in other US College coaches from across the USA to work with the crews.

As a start for understanding the concept of "integral coaching," it is helpful to recognize that the rowing stroke is a cyclical whole unit and also recognize that our body, the rowing stroke, nature and our world, function optimally as a whole. The body, in combination with the mind and the spirit, forms a complete system. The total organism moves up and down the slide as a unit with a strong connection to the shell and the oar/blade action. The many parts blend into a whole stroke which represents a beautiful metaphor and perfect parallel to the holism of life and nature on this planet with its solid entry, the steady middle passage, and quiet exit.

Awareness and care of our immediate environment is important for our sculling and our life beyond sculling. My memory recalls how immersed I was in the wind, rain, and waves of Toronto harbor on my way to race on the quiet waters of the lagoon of Toronto Island. The home course of the legendary

Hanlan. Before racing, the fragile shell had to be beached and emptied of water, yet I recall feeling entirely at ease in my environment. When the sculler develops this state of mind he sees his sculling, the environment, the world as one, and as a whole. Then he is transformed to another level of athletic intelligence, in his sculling, and in his being. All of us in this beautiful sport can become "conservationists and environmentalists."

Integration insures the correct balance between the intensive and relaxed states of movement. You should have a certain amount of tension in the body on the recovery and a certain amount of relaxation in the movements during the drive. The release action in rowing, where five movements are performed in rapid succession to make the motion appear as one, is a wonderful example of unity and integration. The stroke is the epitome of wholeness with its continuous, cyclical and elliptical action, With its rounded continuous edges at each end of the slide bed, the cycle seems to mirror the workings of our beautiful universe in its constant changes and interdependent movements. The rowing stroke touches upon both the exterior and interior dimensions of the athlete, so the process of "integral coaching" begins with the athlete's rowing experience.

In further support of integration, we know that the entry movements in sculling are more effective when the athlete combines the power from the legs, trunk and arms. Consequently on the drive, the integration of body movements creates an effortless, level run to the shell paralleling our flow and an integrative life in this world. The sequential joint action of the total body stride is integrated with the summated forces from the trunk, legs, and arms.

This requires a strong shoulder girdle so that the resultant shoulder/arm draw is a smooth transition from extension to flexion. Our winter strength program should reflect this need for strong shouders. The fluid arm draw is one of the most difficult movements in rowing. It requires a steady pull of the blade through the water at blade width depth, in coordination with the steady leg and trunk pressure. The relationship of blade to body is solid at all points in the cycle. Simulation exercises help immensely to develop this fluid arm action.The power displacement and shifting of weight from the entry to the release is also similar to the swings in baseball and golf, illustrating a connection between the various sports. In each sport, the athlete "strides on the drive" with a powerful integrated movement. The two Roberts, Fitzpatrick and Pearce, understood the summation of forces principle.

Hank Aaron, the baseball great, was a perfect example of this integrated power. He hit over 750 home runs during his carrer. He had a slight stature, but he summated the forces of his trunk, legs and arms with his integrated swinging action. In contrast, Frank Howard, a contemporary of Aaron, and a very large athlete, hit 382 home runs in his career employing a fragmented, sequenced and awkward stride — a step, then a swing. He lacked Aaron's foundation of flow and wholeness in his swing.

On the question of wholeness and fragmentation, the quantum physicist David Bohm writes,

> "...some might say: Fragmentation of cities, religions, political systems, conflict in the form of wars, general violence, fraticide , etc., are

the reality. Wholeness is only an ideal,
toward which we should perhaps strive. But
this is not what is being said here. Rather,
what should be said is that wholeness is
what is real, and that fragmentation is man's
action guided by his illusory perception....So
what is needed is for man to give attention to
his habit of fragmentary thought, to be aware
of it, and thus bring it to an end. Man's
approach to reality may then be whole, and
so the response will be whole."[33]

For Bohm, wholeness is experiencing reality in our bodies, in nature, in thought and in life; fragmentation, in the form of various conflicts, we mistakenly think is reality. So, the emphasis on and realization of wholeness has the potential to enrich our coaching and our lives. As stated earlier, it is critical that we spend significant amount of time each day embraced by the wholeness of nature. Bohm felt that fragmentation in large part was caused by our thinking of objects as separate entities and not as part of a larger world. He also felt that the structure of our language led to fragmentation. This compartmentalization is evident in rowing when the coach explains the drive phase in segments of legs, trunk and arms action. Might it be better to think of the concentrated and cooordinated power of these segments applying effective force at each point in the drive? This interprets the rowing stroke as a smooth transition from extension of the arms at the entry to flexion of the arms at the release.

---

[33] David Bohm, *Wholeness and the Implicate Order* (New York, NY: Routledge Press, 1980).

Thus Bohm envisions reality as a process that is like a flowing stream. The parts of the stream, waves, ripples , splashes etc., have no independent existence — they are simply the stream. Bohm's perspective has immediate application in a crew where the individual members have to feel the link to the person rowing in front of them and behind them. Then the crew member is a whole and the crew is whole. For the coach, Bohm's pronouncements are a meaningful and helpful perspective on science, on philosophy, and have significant implications for rowing. Addressing another perspective on sport were Henry Bugbee's concerns expressed in his probing work, *The Inward Morning* that "the athletic atmosphere can be asphyxiating."[34] Much of this toxic atmosphere comes from too much effort by the athlete. Fitzpatrick's advice of "pulling what you can handle" countered the extreme effort of the athlete who was trying too hard. Leonard DeFrancesco, a former Tennis Coach at William Smith, used almost similar terms when he urged his players "that less is more and don't kill the ball." If you kill the ball your stroke is frantic and the rhythm of the stroke is destroyed. Some of the smooth stroking tennis players include Roger Federer, Bjorn Borg, Pete Sampras, Rod Laver, Ken Rosewall, Kim Clister, and Monica Seles. Similarly, baseball players Hank Aaron, Ted Williams and Babe Ruth had beautiful effortless swings.

The great Indian philosopher, Krishnamurti, emphasizes the importance of this holistic method when he writes, "We have to observe the whole field...

---

[34] Henry Bugbee, *The Inward Morning: A Philosophical Exploration in Journal Form* (Athens, GA: University of Georgia Press, 1999).

And these fragmentary energies are wasting our total energy."[35] The whole field for the sculler includes the body, shell, oars and water. We must be able see the forest as well as the individual trees. Georg Feuerstein further elaborates on this concept when he writes,

> "The integral attitude is a disposition that favors quiet and silence over haste and noise; spontaneity over goal-directed thinking; compassion and loving kindness over lust for power and manipulation; inner harmony and balance over mechanical organizing; unsentimental tolerance over prejudice; authenticity over blind conformism; delight in inner growth over fear of change; acceptance of life and death over mere avoidance."[36]

Fitzpatrick would remind his scullers that no matter how they performed, the sun would always come up the next morning on the horizon. He put the sport in perspective to life.

Knowledge of science alone is not enough for effective coaching. Ken Wilber cautions that we avoid this "flatland thinking," the one-dimensional approach which occurs when we rely only on science and the external, objective world and neglect to account for the activity of the subjective and the

---

[35] J. Krishnamurti, *The Wholeness of Life* (San Francisco, CA: Harper & Row, 1979).

[36] Georg Feuerstein, *Lucid Waking: Mindfulness and the Spiritual Potential of Humanity* (Rochester, VT: Inner Traditions International, 1997).

internal world.[37] The overemphasis on the value of
the ergometer score for an athlete's development is
an egregious example of this type of thinking by the
coach.

Both science and experiential wisdom
comprise the major sources of knowledge for the
coach and athlete. Therefore, integrative coaching
includes the various sciences, physiology,
psychology, training methodology, biomechanics,
nutrition, movement training, and mind science.
Canadian National Team Strength Trainer, Ed
McNeely observes that "humans are complex systems
and while coaching we tend to look at the pieces.
Optimal development of an athlete can only occur
when we realize that every system in the body effects
every other system, and the body parts function best
in a cooperative mode. The coach is encouraged to
look outside the box, and treat the athlete as an
integrated system of physiological, mechanical,
social, and psychological components."[38]

Thus, integrative training encompasses the
sciences, the meditative practices and the various
forms of cross-training including: flexibility training,
yoga, the jumping rope for rhythm, coordination and
timing, running with three modes of hill runs,
fartleks, long slow distance work, as well as body
weights and free weights for strength training. All of
these are done with a progressive system of training
and maintaining throughout the year. The rowing
should include aerobic, threshold and anaerobic

[37] Ken Wilber, *Integral Psychology: Consciousness, Spirit, Psychology, Therapy* (Boston, MA: Shambhala, 2000).

[38]Ed McNeely, *Integral Coaching* (presented at the The Joy of Sculling, Saratoga Springs, NY, 2007).

modes in addition to simulation drills, speed work, quickness drills and easy speed workouts.

The coaching is also enhanced by the science of the mind achieved through the study and practice of psychology. Consequently, modern psychology is augmented with meditative practices and the reading of timeless works of wisdom, that have an extensive history in both western and eastern literature. The psychological aspect of the skill learning is often overlooked. It entails an evolutionary development of the coach and athlete's consciousness as the skill evolves to higher levels of complexity that include and transcend previous levels of understanding, being and doing.

The central premise of the integral approach is that everyone, all disciplines and fields of study, have some measure of the truth, so no information should be discounted. Every piece of information has some degree of value at some level of the athlete's training. The wise rowing coach uses different sources of information from the old English Orthodoxy to Fairbairn to more modern concepts at the appropiate level and stage in the athlete's development. As an example, the Orthodox practice of slowing down before the entry is an excellent method to improve the timing but you would never race this way. So, it is helpful if we identify different levels of technique- beginning, intermediate, and advanced- for each athlete.

Ken Wilber identifies the diffent levels of consciousness, so that all knowledge has value depending on the level that it is to be applied. For example, Wilber would see Freud's work as appropiate at one level of consciousness and Carl Jung's teachings at a deeper level of consciousness.

"the result is a significant movement of
ess from "me" to "we" to "us" to "all of
cultural shift from an egocentric to
world centric and hopefully
levels and viewpoints."[39] This
progression through the major levels is a roadmap
that begins with empathy for the self and proceeds to
the family, the community, the nation, the world and
finally to the planet. The mind becomes more
expansive, free and open. This is a model for living a
life of concern for others that the coach and athlete
must try to embrace; it is rooted in wholeness. "True
unity in the individual and between man and nature,
as well as between man and man, can arise only in a
form of action that does not attempt to fragment the
whole of reality."[40]

Empathy is the main source for developing the
spirit in the self and in the team. According to Mary
Gordon, "Empathy is integral to solving conflict in the
family, the schoolyard, the boardroom, and the war
room." The athlete who has empathy is less critical of
himself and his teammates. The coach seeks and
tries to instill this quality of empathy and mental
expansion in the athlete and the team. This is the
path to higher skill levels and a more powerful inner
state of being. With this humanistic coaching
approach sport has the potential for doing good in
the world. The history of sport and specifically rowing
has produced some excellent coaches who used this
humanistic approach informally in their training

---

[39] Ken Wilber, *Sex, Ecology, Spirituality: The Spirit of Evolution*, in The Collected Works of Ken Wilber (Boston, MA: Shambhala, 2000).

[40] Bohm, *Wholeness and the Implicate Order*.

practices,and achieving one or more of the major levels of consciousness mentioned above.

The virtues of the self include stillness rather than movement; silence in place of speech; being rather than becoming; and the importance of inner essence over outer substance. These values apply to both the coach and the athlete. With this type of method/philosophy, the learning process cannot be hurried. The coach is working with nature, human nature in the broadest sense - mind, body and spirit development (which respectively correspond to the technical, physical and mental aspects of training.) With this approach, the learning process is enjoyable and there is a high degree of self-realization on the part of the student and the teacher. The exploration of one's limits and personal growth are stressed culminating in an effective performance model in contrast to a more competitive model. If the athlete learns to perform at his peak ability because of an expanded consciousness, then he will achieve his best competitive results possible.

Lao Tzu on self mastery wrote:

> *Those who know others are intelligent;*
> *Those who know themselves have insight.*
> *Those who masters others have force;*
> *Those who master themselves have strength.*[41]

The scope of the training format requires depth and span, and should consider both the interior and exterior dimensions of each athlete for optimizing his

---

[41] R. L. Wing, *The Tao of Power* (Garden City, NY: Dolphin Book, 1986).

development. Both the coach and the athlete are transformed from the study of the wisdom literature. I suggest the athletes begin by reading Eugen Herrigel's little book, *Zen in the Art of Archery*. This approach requires experience with meditative or yoga-type practices or some other concentrative activity to embrace the whole organism - the body, the mind and the spirit. For the coach and athlete, these mental, physical and spiritual experiences have a deeper purpose that optimize the individual's performance and personal development. This type of coaching approach includes all aspects of training, monitoring and interrelationships with the athlete.

Gerhardt Schmolinsky, editor of the East German book, *Track and Field*, wrote,

"The level of physical ability is great importance, but is only one factor. Not every agile and strong athlete learns a new movement in a short time; we know that versatile athletes acquire new skills more quickly, due to a special faculty of the cerebral cortex known as 'plasticity.' Plasticity is the ability to create new complexes of conditioned reflexes and to modify existing ones. The more complexes there are, the greater is the plasticity.

A guiding principle can be deduced from this for the training of technique, the more varied and numerous the dynamic stereotypes which an athlete has acquired through his many-sided athletic training, the greater is the

capacity to learn new movements and modify known patterns.[42]

So, the athlete should be exposed a variety of training methods in order to insure the development of plasticity. This is important for both the coach and the athlete to understand.

It is imperative that the coach be an active participant in this type of comprehensive training in guiding the athlete. He develops and experiences the process with the athlete. Our holistic selves and the level of our empathy undergo great evolutionary development. Ultimately our being evolves beyond the individual self to eventually encompass the environment, so that in sculling the total body blends with the oars the shell and the water in a rhythmic dance of flow.

The integral approach is ambitious and demands a comprehensive effort both intellectually and physically from the coach and the athlete. Eventually the philosophy invades and embraces one's total being with a lifetime commitment and it enhances the enjoyment, education and challenges for athletic training and coaching. It represents a general overlay of the more specific levels that include matter, body, mind, soul and spirit. Integral thought has only evolved as discipline in the last 25 years, in large part due to the profound and prodigious work of great philosophers, scientists and depth psychologists, such as A.H. Almaas, Sri Aurobindo, Allan Combs, Henri Bergson, David Bohm, Duane Elgin, Jean Gebser, Jiddu Krishnamurti, Scott

---

[42] Gerhardt Schmolinsky and Deutsche Hochschule für Körperkultur Leipzig. Wissenschaftsbereich Leichtathletik., *Track and Field: Text-Book for Coaches and Sports Teachers* (Berlin: Sportverlag, 1978).

Russell Sanders, Teilhard de Chardin, and Ken Wilber, whose works illustrate the presence and greater need for integration in our world.

Flow

Flow and enjoyment of the sport is an important product of mental training. When the athlete's mind and body are relaxed, focused and concentrated in the present moment, fluid movement or "flow" occurs. We witness specific evidence of "flow" in the individual movements of the athlete - a stroke, a swing, a stride. In rowing, total integration of the body movements with the shell, blades and water, along with a heightened awareness and concentration of the athletes's mind and spirit produce "flow." The development of this type of action in rowing is greatly assisted by smooth movements at each end of the stroke (reversibility principle). These same individual and physical qualities of the athlete surface in the dynamics of concerted team action, i.e. the run of the shell.

In the foreword to *Tao Te Ching*, Stephen Mitchell writes: "A good athlete can enter a state of body awareness in which the right stroke or the right movement happens by itself, effortlessly, without any interference of the conscious will. The game plays the game; the poem writes the poem; we can't tell the dancer from the dance."[43] Ultimately the coach and athlete become one through their work together on the development of fluid technique. The critical factors for achieving *flow* include consistent stroke length, accurate blade depth and even pressure on the blade face during the drive phase. The simulation exercises are extremely helpful in developing these skills in the crew.

---

[43] Stephen Mitchell, *Tao Te Ching* (New York, NY: Harper, 1988).

Art Wilmarth, a former Yale lightweight oarsman and currently a Professor of Law at George Washington University, recently wrote this letter recalling his college rowing experience.

> *"The integration of philosophical, spiritual and psychological insights with physical training has been a hallmark of your coaching career. I always appreciated your emphasis on technique and swing as essential components of power (as opposed to brute force). I'm sure that I could never have succeeded in a rowing program that emphasized quantitative measures of force (e.g., the ergometer). I remember watching other rowers working on ergometers (which were just beginning to be used at the end of my rowing days at Yale). Many of the rowers distorted their technique just to generate a few more revolutions of the ergometer -- I couldn't see much sense in that. My strongest memories of rowing are of practices or races where the boat was truly running out and we could hear the gurgling of the water under the shell. During those times I definitely felt "in the zone" and there was very little consciousness of "work" -- instead, I felt the coordination of our collective efforts and the harmony of the shell with the water and the surrounding environment."[44]*

Art has never lost his appreciation for flow.

We can make our skills more automatic and "race proof" with consistent and concentrated

---

[44] Personal Correspondence, 2010.

practice and monitoring. With experience we can become more aware of what we are doing while we are doing it. However, as stated earlier, this mental state can be accelerated with the regular practice of meditation. When we combine the high levels of skill with equally high levels of consciousness, we can achieve flow and experience peak performance. If the peak performance is consistent, then we have a "plateau performance."[45] Thus, these altered states become altered traits with concentrated and consistent meditative practice. Note, however, the mastery of mental skills can begin at the same time as the mastery physical skills (see Figure 3.1). The mental skills assist with the progress of the physical skills at all stages of development of each component.

Figure 3.1 The Flow Staircase

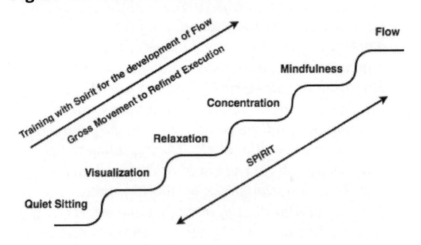

Duane Elgin, a transpersonal or evolutionary psychologist, has this observation, "*Flow* consciousness has long been recognized by athletes

---

[45] Daniel Goleman, "Taming Destructive Emotions," *Tricycle* 2003.

when they achieve a high level of concentration and synchronization."[46] *Flow* consciousness is paradoxical in that it often requires great effort and concentration to achieve a result that is seemingly effortless and spontaneous. The long distance runner Dr. George Sheehan states "that after a half hour of running I see myself not as an individual but as part of the universe."[47] With efficiency we move beyond effort as an individual and find stillness in the wholeness of our being. Here is how Steve McKinney described his experience of breaking the world downhill ski record: "I discovered the middle path of stillness within speed, calmness within fear, and I held it longer and quieter than ever before."[48]

Moshe Feldenkrais, an expert in the field of movement, stated that it is important to learn how to turn strenuous movements into good ones, that is, into movements that are first of all effective but also smooth and easy. This takes miles of rowing and hours of intensive drilling on specific parts of the stroke cycle to accomplish. Feeling the movement, the flow of the body and the run of the shell must be done in a relaxed and informal way. Our physical suppleness developed out of the boat must be carried into the shell. This economy of motion must be both a state of mind and of body — "the lazy athlete." Hockey player Gordie Howe of the Detroit Red Wings immediately comes to mind with his strong, effortless

---

[46] Elgin, *Awakening Earth: Exploring the Evolution of Human Culture and Consciousness*.

[47] George Sheehan, *Running and Being: The Total Experience* (New York, NY: Slmon and Schuster, 1978).

[48] Elgin, *Awakening Earth: Exploring the Evolution of Human Culture and Consciousness*.

strides developed during boyhood on the frozen rivers of his native Saskatchewan. Witnessing Don Schollander in the Yale pool in the late 1960s upon his return to school, after his extraordinary gold medal performances in the 1964 Tokyo Olympics, was a sight of great beauty. He personified effortlessness. We saw these same qualities in the two gold medal eights in the 2008 Olympics. In sculling, the development of this type of action is greatly assisted with smooth movements at each end of the stroke (reversibility).

Posture also plays an important part in developing *flow*, beginning with the relaxed holding of the oar. F. Mathias Alexander, a famous Australian practitioner of posture at the turn of the 19th century wrote, "the delicate poise of the head, neck and torso allows a high degree of sensitivity and harmony, and true harmony with an instrument (shell and oar) must begin with harmony of self."[49] Alexander was reacting to the stiff Victorian posture of the body of his day. One of the best way to develop this harmony of self is through the meditative practices.

All of this involves hours of practice, openness to change, and a deep awareness of both the exterior and interior qualities of our athletic being. When we speak of practice, we refer to yoga, rowing at slow motion, good technique in weight training and body weight exercises, core-training, rope jumping for rhythm, careful attention to our running form and finally, good posture for our meditative practices. With good technique in weight lifting, the athlete reinforces his coordination, flow and accuracy. We

---

[49] F. Matthias Alexander, *The Resurrection of the Body* (New York, NY: University Books, 1969).

can observe these superbly coordinated weight lifters every four years at the Olympics.

The diversity and variety in the practice format is critical for learning the physical and mental sensitivity required to be a highly skilled athlete. This is also a balanced and integral approach to training and coaching. Ultimately, the union of these principles enables the athlete and coach to train with spirit towards the goal of *flow* illustrated in Figure 3.1.

The late Paul Fitzgerald, a lifelong friend, a wonderful athlete, and an avid student of golf, made these observations and remarks on reading the *flow* staircase for the first time:

> *"In golf, breath leads to relaxation of both body and mind as you quietly approach the ball; you visualize the shot that must be made. A deep breath leads to relaxation of both body and mind to remove the tension from the swing. Concentration is found in the alignment of the club face, and the focus on grip, stance, and posture. Watch the pros when they prepare to hit their shot and you will see this in their set up. Mindfulness would be found in two ways, as a key "swing thought" for the amateur (the athlete consciously thinks of the various movements), and for an awareness of the target site for the professional who may be beyond "swing thought" as a conscious entity. The "flow" is found in the smooth "tempo" of the swing,*

*and is the result of the confidence acquired
from the lower steps of the staircase."[50]*

This was a beautiful piece of spontaneous thinking and writing by Paul.

Great athletes are able to produce this effective action under competitive conditions. Some of the most prominent examples in rowing during recent times are the winning performances by Ekaterina Karsten in the 1999 Worlds, by Peter Haining in the 1994 Worlds and Xeno Muller's performance in the 1996 Olympics. Additionally, Karsten's winning the gold medal in the same Olympics is another example. Both Karsten and Muller displayed efficient, fluid acceleration over the last 500 meters of their respective gold medal performances. They were able to change their base stroke rating with an "easy speed," and accelerate past their opponents in the final 500 meters of the race because their integrated drives allowed them to flow. Their respective second place opponents were rowing the scull with a fragmented drive.

George Leonard, in his book, *The Transformation*, cites a wonderful example of the *flow* state found in Leo Tolstoy's *Anna Karenina* where he describes Levin's work with the scythe mowing hay.

*"The longer Levin kept moving the more often
he would feel the moments of oblivion when it
would no longer be his arms that were
swinging the scythe, but the scythe itself, like
a body full of life and self-consciousness,
would move forward of its own accord, and
the work would perform itself, accurately and*

---

[50] Personal Correspondence

carefully, as though by magic, without a thought being given to it."[51]

This excellent example of fluid, transcendent action from the literature is easily transferable to rowing. It is reminiscent of my boyhood memories watching the effortless strokes of the workers beside the Canadian National Railway in St.Catharines cutting the long summer grass. They had learned to sustain their effort over a ten hour work day because the flow of their arm action was integrated with their legs and trunk. It was an automatic movement, part of their total being. Similarly, Fitzpatrick cited the example of the loggers in the Northwest using the long cross saw; so sculling is similar to the "sawing wood" action. These examples of *flow* remind us that it is important at times, to leave our "home of thought," and play intuitively.

Former Washington Post sports editor Shirley Povich's recollection of Babe Ruth's batting swing is a vivid example of fluid motion: "...the most striking thing about Ruth at bat was not simply the power that he generated but also the beauty of his swing. He made home run hitting look easy." Povich continued, "There was no violence in the stroke. He put everything into it, but he never looked like he was extending himself. By the time he hit the ball, he had taken a long stride forward and had turned his shoulders and ass and wrists into it, swinging through it. Exquisite timing. I can close my eyes and not only still see the swing but admire it."[52] I think

---

[51] George Burr Leonard, *The Transformation: A Guide to the Inevitable Changes in Humankind* (New York, NY: Delacorte Press, 1972).

[52] William Mack, "The Colossus," *Sports Illustrated* 1998.

that this aspect of Ruth's extensive athleticism is often overlooked when assessing his abilities.

Amy Wettergreen, a 2004 U.S. and Canadian National Champion and a William Smith grad, wrote of her experience with *flow* during a scrimmage in the fall of 1995:

> *"The thing that I remember the most about "flow," and particularly the scrimmage at Syracuse, was the stillness, the ease of movement, the hush that settles over your body and your mind. It is the quiet stillness that frees your mind to focus on the body, the moment, the movement - but by focus, I do not mean that you are trying to get your mind to cooperate. It's more like that you are letting your mind do what it wants to do — to quietly get in tune with your body and respond to the moment. And the body responds without any direction from the mind because both the mind and body are already In The Moment Of FLOW - without direction, without effort. There is a feeling of overwhelming energy that is now at your disposal - like you have tapped into infinite possibility. It feels like you could go on forever - you are limitless, bound by nothing, free to envision what is possible. Free to visualize a perfect performance. And this is where the mental training comes in - all of a sudden, you are in FLOW and you can create the reality of winning because both your mind/body is fully cooperating with this mental image. It becomes the overriding desire of the moment - to fulfill what you have begun, to respond to this heightened state of*

being, to reach full potential, to surpass all expectations of what is possible. All at once, you are manifesting strength, stillness, speed, relaxation, power, synergy, FLOW.'[53]

Amy and her William Smith teammates would experience this phenomenon a number of times in their college rowing.

---

[53] Personal Correspondence, 1995.

The Functional Athlete

"You need the flow of the mind, the body, the blades and the shell. The integration of these four components creates flow on a regular basis in practice and race situations. Coaches and athletes end up achieving one or two of these components, but rarely all four working in harmony."

Jimmy Joy

When athletes operate as a powerful "function" or "ball of energy," they become more than a simple physical structure.[54] Their power originates from stillness, from deep inside themselves, releasing outward through effective limb action. There is no wasted motion and the movements are fluid and powerful. Inner stillness develops with consistent meditative practice and easy concentrated rows on the ergometer during the winter. The athlete is encouraged to monitor the stillness and economy of the body segments during the various phases of the stroke. This efficiency of mind and body is found in outstanding smaller statured athletes such as Peter Antonie, Australia (1992 gold), Pat Turner, Canada (1984 gold), and Laryssa Biesenthal, Canada (1996 silver). These smaller athletes are excellent barometers for human potential and *flow*. Amy Wettergreen, with her slight stature, but tremendous inner resources, was also an example of this type of athlete. Two other outstanding examples of the "functional athlete" were the old and the modern scullers, Ned Hanlan and Peter Haining.

Ned Hanlan, a relatively short person at 5'8", was able to win over 300 sculling races against much

---

[54] Shi Ming, *Mind over Matter: Higher Martial Arts* (Berkeley, CA: North Atlantic Books, 1994).

larger men in the late 19th century. His success can be attributed to his endurace training, his well - timed pendular swing, his coordinated drive of the blade through the water, and his overall watermanship and athleticism. He lived, trained, and played on the waters of Toronto harbor from his Toronto island home.

Haining was listed as one of the best all-time scullers in a 2003 Rowing News article. He displayed *flow* in his World Lightweight Championship victory in 1994 and at the post-race interview exclaimed, "It was like I was on a runaway freight train."[55]

This particular philosophy of the "functional athlete" recognizes the power of the whole athlete - spiritual and mental, as well as physical — internal as well as external. Eugen Herrigel, writing in *Zen in the Art of Archery*, observes "that the bow, the arrow, goal and ego, all melt into one another so that I can no longer separate them."[56] In rowing, this coaching approach facilitates the athlete's realization of optimal potential described in Herrigel's writing. His book is recommended reading for athletes.

Effective, economical and powerful internal and external body movements are synchronized with the oars and the shell. Mihaly Csikszentmihalyi, an expert on "flow," wrote the following explanation of this phenomenon (I have added specific rowing situations stated in the parentheses): "We experience it as a unified flowing from one movement to the next (continuity in the stroke cycle) in which we feel control of our actions (feeling of the movement under

[55] FISA, "Post-Race Interview with Peter Haining," (1994).

[56] Eugen Herrigel, *Zen in the Art of Archery* (New York, NY: Vintage Books, 1989).

control), and in which there is little distinction between self and environment (the shell, oars, water and athlete are one); between stimulus and response (the oars are applied and the shell responds beautifully); or between past, present, and future (there is unity in the appearance of the start, body, and finish of the race of the accomplished sculler/ crew)."[57]

These passages are excellent illustrations of work as effortless, where action and awareness merge, and the movement becomes unconscious. The flow of the body, and its accompanying instrument, an oar, stick, bat or racquet, becomes the external manifestation of internal balance, rhythm and power. The body movements demonstrate a refinement that includes the qualities of relaxation, concentration, and focus. Ken Wilber reminds us that, "in order to master the mind, one must master the body's subtle energies and movements at every stage of development."[58]

---

[57] Mihaly Csikszentmihalyi, "Play and Intrinsic Rewards," *Journal of Humanistic Psychology* 15, no. 3 (1975).

[58] Wilber, *Integral Psychology: Consciousness, Spirit, Psychology, Therapy.*

The Role of the Coach

Seeing — we might say that the whole of life lies in that verb.
Pierre Teilhard de Chardin

Yes, in addition to being a good listener, the coach must be a good observer of the athlete's skills and most importantly, his inner state. Fitzpatrick was constantly reading the athglete's inner state through the athlete's exterior body comportment. He was accutely sensitive to the power of the inner athlete.

Traditionally, the coach establishes the focus for a practice by demonstrating some aspect of the stroke cycle at the beginning of each practice; he serves as a demonstrator in this particular role. In addition to sitting quietly with the team, planning, choreographing and leading the workouts, the coach can assist the athlete's development by exposing the athlete to outside readings from philosophical and spiritual sources. The readings from the "wisdom literature" support, explain and reinforce the importance of such meditative practices. For example, one of the best pieces of writing on anxiety was done by the Dalai Lama in the *Art of Happiness*; I distributed the complete chapter to the team to read. Phil Jackson gives his athletes books to read as well. However, the crew coach, because of the numbers involved, can usually only provide the athletes short handouts from the wisdom literature on a weekly basis. At Hobart-William Smith, it was apparent that the readings assisted the athlete's improvement in the understanding of consciousness. By the end of a four year college career the athlete will have compiled a large booklet of handouts that reflect deep wisdom.

Almost 50 years ago, in the foreword of his book *Athletics: How to be a Champion*, Percy Cerutty, the great Australian track coach, wrote the following:

> *"I freely admit my debt to all the great minds that have gone before, from Plato and Aristotle right through to Newton, Hackenschmidt, and Hoffman, the fathers of the modern world athletics era. I have read widely on all subjects, ranging from Freud to Krishnamurti, Buddha and Jesus, to Carrell, Jeans, and Einstein. What have these hundred or more "authorities", scientists, philosophers, to do with world class athletic performance? I say everything, if the athlete would be a complete man and not merely a physical exponent of some process he may have been gifted with in the first place. The pure "physical" instructor, coach or athlete - if such could be said to exist — could not imagine the realm of ideas that can be applied to high level performance. Indeed, the top performers of the future will increasingly result from the "spirit" and high intelligence (brains of the first order)."*[59]

Cerutty, a lively, spirited coach, was an avid reader of the great works of literature as seen by the excerpt above from his book. He had an expansive consciousness that he shared with his athletes. Cerutty was almost a spiritual coach. By "spiritual," we ascribe to Georg Feuerstein's definition of "any value, thought attitude, impulse, mood, disposition,

---

[59] Percy Wells Cerutty, *Athletics: How to Become a Champion* (London, UK: Stanley Paul, 1960).

bodily comportment, or action which refers to, or is expressive of, the native human orientation of self-transcendence." Great coaches, like Cerutty, could lead their athletes to transcend their normal selves and limits.

Cerutty developed an elaborate philosophy of coaching that was based on Spartanism, or strict discipline and stoicism, or indifference to pain. He labeled his system "Stotan". His most famous student and runner was the great Herb Elliott, the undefeated miler at the 1960 Olympics. Cerutty coached by example, even in his sixties as he led his runners through strenuous weight training sessions and hill runs up large sand dunes at his ocean-side training camp in Portsea, Australia. Cerutty's deep reflection and writing came in advance of the transpersonal psychologists/philosophers of the last half of the 20th century. These thinkers integrate science with consciousness training and foreshadow the application of this integral approach in all areas of life including law, business, science, the arts, and athletics.

Harry Parker, in his mid-seventies, displays a similar but quiet type of leadership by example for his Harvard students. He is not only physically fit but deeply cerebral. One of Parker's exceptional athletes at Harvard was Michael Livingston who wrote an excellent book, *Mental Discipline: The Pursuit of Peak Performance.* He believed in the power of the mind, and his intensive study coupled the impact of science on learning, with his study and practice of Eastern "disciplines of the mind."

Coaches can provide a deeper philosophy and life perspective for the athletes using the ideas of these great thinkers. When Waldemar Cierpinski, the

1976 Olympic marathon champion from East Germany was asked about his coaches, he cited Jörg Ramlow, who gave him an interest in the arts, discussions of literature, the theater, and listening to classical music. Ken Doherty calls this type of learning and teaching, "holistic", where one's education, experience, and practice are integrated.[60] I would also characterize this type of coaching as the indirect approach - "the longest way around is the shortest way home."[61] It is a highly effective philosophy for coaching. Don't take short shortcuts, be thorough.

Phil Jackson, in a similar vein to Cerutty's philosophical studies, writes, "I started exploring a variety of paths. Inspired by *Sunseed*, a film about the search for enlightenment, I began taking yoga classes, reading books about eastern religion, and attending lectures by Krishnamurti, Pir Vilayat Khav, and other spiritual teachers."[62] The readings he provides his players create an understanding of the importance of an integrated approach to training, which includes developing the mind and spirit as well as the body. The readings also emphasize the importance of an expanded mental outlook to training and life. The information from this literature supplies the reader with valuable assistance for finding parallels between the thought of eastern mystics and the qualities that western coaches are seeking in their athletes. The readings from the eastern philosophers, mind science, integral

---

[60] Joy, *The Art of Sculling.*

[61] Basil Liddell-Hart, *Strategy* (New York, NY: Praeger, 1967).

[62] Jackson, *Sacred Hoops: Spiritual Lessons of a Hardwood Warrior.*

psychology, and deep ecology represent a form of mental cross-training for the coach and athlete. For example, how appropiate is Henry David Thoreau's admonition of "Simplify, simplify, simplify"...and Shunryu Suzuki's, "In the beginner's mind there are many possibilities, in the expert's there are none."

For many athletes these readings represent their initial exposure to this type of literature, and consequently, leave an indelible imprint on their educational experience, and subsequently, lead to an expansion of their consciousness. The readings actually provide the athlete an opportunity to take a "right turn" in their lives moving from accumulating more information to experiencing wisdom. This "right turn" can have a significant effect on both the athlete's life and his athleticism. In some ways we in the west have been half educated with concentrating solely on western literature and source material, but that is changing. Now, a whole new world of eastern literature and wisdom is available to us.

The emphasis of this type of coaching approach is clearly the individual's development both as as a person and as an athlete. So any performance concerns are primary with the process. Winning is secondary. It is helpful to be reminded of the words of Chuang Tzu, the ancient Chinese Taoist master in his poem, The Need to Win:

When an archer is shooting for nothing
He has all his skill.
If he shoots for a brass buckle
He is already nervous.
If he shoots for a prize of gold
He goes blind
Or he sees two targets -
He is out of his mind!

His skill has not changed. But the prize
Divides him. He cares.
He thinks more of winning
Than of shooting -
And the need to win
Drains him of power. [63]

The wisdom of Chuang Tzu reminds me of Derek Porter's objective for his inital race in the men's single event at the World Championships in 1993, after stroking the gold medal eight in 1992. His goals were simply to scull well and try to make the top twelve. When he made the top twelve his objectives were to scull well and make the finals. When he made the finals his objectives were to scull well and medal. In the final at the 1000 meter mark he found that he was close to a medal. At the 500 meter mark he found that he was in third place and only then did he think of winning, which he accomplished. Similar to Thoreau, Porter's approach was simple, and like Suzuki, he was open to possibilities - he had a beginner's mind.

------

[63] Thomas Merton, *The Way of Chuang Tzu* (Boston, MA: Shambhala, 1992).

In the late 1980s, then Vice-President and now the current President of the Coaching Association of Canada, John Bales, related to me the story of East German officials making a trip to India to learn how the Indian philosophies could be applied in sport training. The great Indian holistic mystic and philosopher Sri Aurobindo had a sport institute as part of his ashram in Pondicherry, India. Aurobindo was deeply committed to developing what he referred to as the "vital" or quiet center of our being. So, Integral Yoga - breathing, posture and meditation - was central to his teaching and method of practice. Besides Aurobindo, the two other learned Indian 20th century practitioners of holistic philosophy encompassing the body, mind, and spirit, were Gandhi and Krishnamurti. I consider these three gentlemen intellectual, spiritual, and physical athletes of the highest order. Yes, think about it, they were athletes, as their bodies and minds were extremely fit. They lived, breathed, and practiced their humanistic philosophy and the three of them were serious athletic walkers. This quality of inner quiet can be employed everyday in all sorts of situations, as well as for meeting the demands and stresses of competition.

As described in Peter Hart's, *The Somme: The Darkest Hour on the Western Front*, the bravest, most reliable and focused men under fire in that most devastating of World War I battles displayed strong evidence of this same quiet inner calm.[64] Incidentally, at the final battle of the Somme on 13 November 1916, the rowing world lost one of its quiet leaders,

---

[64] Peter. Hart, *The Somme: The Darkest Hour on the Western Front* (New York, NY: Penguin Books, 2008).

F.S. Kelly, when he was cut down by machine gun fire. He was a Diamond Sculls winner, Henley course record holder and an Olympic Gold medalist. At the height of the Henley Royal Regatta in 1910, Kelly reflected poetically, "On an evening such as this was, all fragrance from the riverside gardens hangs over the surface of the water and one sculls from one scent to another."[65]

Max Picard, in his thoughtful book, *The World of Silence*, writes, "If there is no substance of silence within, the contradictions of one's own personality are exposed to analysis and discussion. Happiness and contentment vanish and humour ceases...Man is better able to endure things hostile to his own nature, things that use him up, if he has the silent substance within."[66] Sri Aurobindo expresses a similar philosophy, "It is only the weak who are agitated; as soon as one becomes truly strong, one is peaceful, calm, quiet, and one has the power of endurance to face the adverse waves which come rushing from the outside in the hope of disturbing one. This true quietude is always a sign of force. Calmness belongs to the strong."[67] Reading passages from the works of these great Indian philosophers, further demonstrating connection of ideas and thoughts on life through the world's many cultures.

---

[65] F.S. Kelly, *The Diaries of F.S. Kelly* (Canberra, AUS: National Library of Australia, 2006).

[66] Max Picard, *The World of Silence* (Wichita, KS: Eighth Day Press, 2002).

[67] A. S. Dalai, *Powers Within: Selections from the Works of Sri Aurobindo and the Mother* (Ojai, CA: Institute of Integral Psychology, 2000).

These qualities are often visible in many of our champion athletes and heroes. I am reminded of Robert Mills from Nova Scotia, who was the bronze medalist in the 1984 Olympics single scull event. Bob was a quiet man, with a wonderful sense of humor, and had tremendous inner resources and strength. His Olympic success was achieved after undergoing a gruelling and extremely difficult selection process for the Canadian team. He exemplified the qualities extolled by Aurobindo.

When the coach recognizes the importance of integration, process, mastery, quiet reflection and *flow*, the athlete is more likely to be exposed to this type of concentration training. This "most effective form of action" by the team has to be facilitated by a coach. The coach serves as an effective facilitator by being integrative, meditative and process-centered in his or her coaching practice. Futhermore, the coach plays multiple roles in the implementation of the training plan including knowledge worker, choreographer, leader, catalyst and wellspring. It is critical for the athletes, the team, the sport and especially for the community that the coach becomes a fully integrated partner in the meditative activity with his athletes. The philosophy of an integrated program clarifies the ultimate objective of a mental training program, which is the total development of the athlete and coach and the experiencing of *flow*.

Joy of Sculling

Summary

The player of the inner game comes to value the art of relaxed concentration above all other skills; he discovers a true basis of self — confidence; and he learns that the secret of winning any game lies in not trying to hard. He aims at the kind of spontaneous performance which occurs only when the mind is calm and seems at one with the body, which finds its own surprising ways to surpass its own limits again and again.

Timothy W. Gallwey

It is very easy to say that you are going to meditate, but difficult to discipline yourself to remain patient and stay with the practice daily. I offer a word of caution to look not for immediate benefits, but to fully engage in the evolutionary process of mind and posture development; it takes time. In this way, the growth of our meditative skills reflects the improvements we should experience in our physical fitness and technical skills. Meditative training facilitates our understanding and practice of economy in our body movements. It is a holistic process involving our total being. Through drilling, the total body movements evolve to higher levels of subtle motion, so it is important for the coach to practice, to refine and then to demonstrate these finer movements to the athlete. At the same time the levels of thinking and knowing evolve simultaneously. The final stage of this development is what Csikszentmihalyi refers to as *flow*: "the holistic sensation present when we act with total involvement in which action follows upon action according to an internal logic which seems to need no conscious intervention on our part."[68] At this point, the coach and crew or athlete become one.

This "internal logic" or intuition recalls a story told to me by my own coach, Bob Fitzpatrick. During a practice Coach Fitzpatrick reached for the megaphone to make a comment to a sculler. The sculler observed Bob's movement and immediately made the targeted technical adjustment without a word spoken. According to the impeccable Fitzpatrick, this amazing communication occurred on two more occasions during the practice, a beautiful example of intuitive sculling and coaching.

The body and mind do evolve and change with consistent training: as coaches we witness the refinement of physical movements and observe the mind reaching higher levels of consciousness. These developments accelerate when one integrates meditative practices into the technical and physical training plans. At the macro level, Teilhard de Chardin saw the evolution of the universe as the development of matter becoming more complex along with higher states of consciousness. It is imperative that you embrace the change. Teilhard recognized that even the mountains change over time. In rowing, the sculler's skills begin to appear simple and fluid with time, but the reality is that they have become

[68] Csikszentmihalyi, "Play and Intrinsic Rewards."

more complex. At the same time, the sculler's awareness, concentration and mindfulness have all reached higher levels of development. So at some point Teilhard de Chardin's concept of matter (the sculling skills) and consciousness (meditative practice) converge, and you have a highly developed athlete who manifests *flow*.

Externally, the dynamic posture improves, the movements become more automatic, the breathing becomes systematic and the athlete's consciousness becomes more intuitive. He simply knows what to do and how to move. He is completely organic. Thus Teilhard's macro theory of evolution and complexity of matter and consiousness converging, parallels the development of the exceptional sculler.

Keep in mind, the first step is to recognize the need to slow down and to experience quiet time and stillness in the mind and within the physical movement. This develops our ability to listen and to observe. We observe our body, our thoughts, and our emotions. In doing so, we remain in the present moment and reduce the occurrence of scattered thinking. We are more relaxed and focused as the mental training is integrated with our daily technical and physical practices, ultimately creating better performance and body discipline.

The more complex the movement skills become, the more the movement achieves a subtle, disciplined and fluid look to it. If you are diligent and consistent in your practice, you will eventually begin to witness a change in your mind as well as changes in your body. You become more relaxed, more patient, more detached from everyday distractions and more consistent in your performance. Your movements will be less rushed, more controlled, balanced, rhythmic, more economical, and will have the quality of stillness. You are mentally aware of your body's movements while you are performing them. It is essential that you make time for some form of mental practice each day throughout the training year. Don't get discouraged, because it is not an easy process. You begin to appreciate that the mental practice comprises a part of your daily training program. It is also important that you try to incorporate these practices and qualities into your daily living situations as much as possible.

Sugar Ray Robinson commented that once a fighter has trained to a certain level, his techniques and responses become almost reflexive. "You don't think. It's all instinct. If you stop to think, you're gone."[69] So in sculling we don't need to set our body, or prepare for our entry movements in the shell; we simply must work for being more instinctual, more fluid, reflexive, and more economical. Physicist David Bohm wrote, "In nature nothing remains constant. Everything is in a perpetual state of transformation, motion, and change."[70] So, the sculling stroke must be a continuous motion or pendular as Hanlan envisaged it.

We see further evidence of this from world champions in every sport. Kurt Browning, the four time men's world champion in figure skating, characterized Sarah Hughes during the 2002 Winter Olympics as "a young girl who works on instinct."[71]

---

[69] Robinson and Anderson, *Sugar Ray: The Sugar Ray Robinson Story.*

[70] David Bohm, *Causality and Chance in Modern Physics* (London, UK: Routledge & Kegan, 1957).

[71] Kurt Browning, 2002. *Olympic Commentary on Sarah Hughes.*

Her movements were extremely fluid. When you are older you think too much. Her goal was simply to skate well and enjoy the skating.

Ken Wilber's interpretation of mind evolution sees this development in the athlete as an integration of refined body movement developing into refined consciousness or spirit (see Figure 3.1). This occurs after hours of accurate drilling, closely monitored by the coach. Personally, the memory of this development is always with me as I recall how the wrist action at the release/feather position evolved under the stress of high stroke rate drills.

Eventually, we expand the level of our consciousness beyond ourselves, beyond our team, beyond our community, to a greater awareness of our total environment. When we reach this point we are no longer ego-logical but rather thoroughly eco-logical in our outlook. We are part of the "living universe." The long distance runner Dr. George Sheehan wrote, "after a half hour of running I see myself not as an individual but as part of the universe."[72]

Outside reading assists this development, as explained in the section on the role of the coach. Guided readings helps us to become less fragmented and more holistic in ourselves and in our worldview; this level of our consciousness has a positive effect on our ability to achieve *flow*, peak experience and peak performance. We are slowing down, less busy and living life with a higher level of quality by being aware of each moment. Our rowing reaches a much higher levels of energy and intensity. Our deep awareness and understanding of these practices

---

[72] Sheehan, *Running and Being: The Total Experience.*

leads to consistent, relaxed, focused, and economical performances on race day. The layout of mental training develops into a simple pattern from the beginning: quiet sitting, through visualization/simulation exercises, to the incorporation of relaxation practices and in the later stages, the use of intensive concentration and mindfulness drills to aid in the final development of mental and physical flow. As our body flows, and our mind becomes more intuitive, and our spirit becomes an integrative force in the our practice and racing, we enjoy and live at plateau experience. To this end, it is important to recognize that the automobile and the various exercising machines lead the athlete away from his magical self. "The magical structure of consciousness is the deeply buried part of us that is characterized by its egolessness, its timelessness and spacelessness, its pointlike unitary world, its playfulness, and its connection to nature."[73] Are these not the qualities found in the superior athlete?

The integrity we perceive in nature is our own birthright. We swim in the one and only stream of life. By recognizing that we are part of this vast, subtle, ancient order, we may be restored to wholeness.[74]

So it is important to live more in the outdoors, every day, in every type of weather conditions. Nature and consciousness need to be connected at every

---

[73] Georg Feuerstein, *Structures of Consciousness: The Genius of Jean Gebser-an Introduction and Critique* (Lower Lake, CA: Integral Publishing, 1987).

[74] Scott Russell Sanders, *A Conservationist Manifesto* (Bloomington, IN: Indiana University Press, 2009).

possible opportunity throughout the year. The great Czech runner, Emil Zatopek stated his attitude to training in adverse conditions: "Whether it is raining, snowing, sleet, or hail, it does not matter. I run free and enjoy the feeling of power in each stride."[75] So, in the 1990s, the Hobart and William Smith athletes were subjected to the rigors of the western New York winters every day, with long distance runs, fartleks, or hills; they were expected to adopt Zatopek's philosophy and be Vikings! By connecting with nature we attempt to transform our sclerotic consciousness and become more open, flexible and adaptable.

Sculling is a great sport, and a beautiful, fluid movement of grace and power when executed properly. If we are going participate in this sport, then it is important to explore the marrow of the athlete - the inner sculler. Ultimately, is this not the responsibility of both the coach and the athlete?

There is endless potential in each athlete that needs to be mined and fostered by the coach. Mastery of the five subtle movements of the release and follow through, is the foundation for the well timed easy swing of the trunk forward. This refined trunk action transforms into the unconscious, effortless glide, a critical skill in the overall structure of the cycle. This statement is almost a metaphor for the book - the development of refining a skill to the point of it being an intuitive action The resultant flow becomes part of the athlete's education and his approach to life beyond his competitive years. Consciousness and skill development are worthy objectives for both the

---

[75] Statement by Emil Zatopek, the 5k, 10k and Olympic Marathon Champion in 1952.

athlete and the coach that require patience, creativity, dedicated practice, and commitment.

Notes & Suggested Readings

From *The Old Coach*

Robert Fitzpatrick spent over 50 years in rowing as a sculler and coaching from 1917 to 1971. He was coached in his native Nova Scotia by John O'Neill of Boston who was also the coach of Frank Greer, the Olympic Champion in 1904. Fitzpatrick later served as Bob Pearce's coach from 1930 to 1932, setting a record in 1928 Olympics that would not be broken until the 1976 Olympics. In 1967, Pearce's native Australia recognized him as the outstanding Australian athlete among all sports in the first 200 years of the country's existence. The 2003 July issue of Rowing News cited Pearce as one of the 10 best scullers in rowing history. Pearce's sculling epitomized power, an effortless stroke, mental concentration, and mental awareness; he is the "Babe Ruth" of sculling.

From Bob Pearce, English Orthodoxy, and Steve Fairbairn, Bob Fitzpatrick was able to formulate an integrated sculling technique. The movements were smooth, rhythmic, and powerfully efficient. The evolution of Fitzpatrick's eclectic technique demonstrated his openness to new ideas and his ability to change. Consequently his athletes sculled with a flat wrist action, level shoulders, impeccable seat-blade timing, and with total mental awareness of the stroke cycle. He remained an avid student of fine sculling, the mind, and of life until his death in 1971.

From *An Introduction to Consciousness*

Readings on recognizing the patterns of our fragmented living:

- Sam Keen, *Learning to Fly.* "Schizophrenic assumptions that governed my life and my practice." Pages 6-7.
- J. Krishnamurti, *Freedom from the Known.* "We live in fragments..." Page 30.
- J. Krishnamurti, *Freedom, Love, and Action.* Pages 17-23.
- Ken Wilber, *A Theory of Everything: An Integral Vision for Business, Politics, Science, and Spirituality.* "Fragmentation at the leading edge..." Page 2.

Readings on recognizing the need to slow down and quiet the mind:

- Eknath Easwaren, *Take Your Time.* Chapter 2, "Slowing Down".
- Eknath Easwaren, *Take Your Time.* "Take Your Time...Slowing Down" Pages 11-34, 35-62.
- J. Krishnamurti, *The Light in Oneself.* "Observing From a Quiet Mind." Pages 78-83.

Readings on recognizing the importance of silence for listening, observing and learning:

- J. Krishnamurti, *Meeting in Life.* Pages 71-74.
- Shi Ming, *Mind over Matter.* Page 127.

From *The Process*

Readings on Quiet Sitting:

- J. Krishnamurti, *The First and Last Freedom*. "On the Stillness of Mind." Pages 277-279.
- J. Krishnamurti, *The Light in Oneself*. "Observing from a Quiet Mind." Pages 78-83.

Readings on Visualization:

- Chungliang Al Huang & J. Lynch, *Thinking Body, Dancing Mind*. Pages 52-58 & 16-22.
- Christmas Humphries, *Concentration and Meditation*. "Visualization." Pages 59-61.
- Denise McCluggage, *Centered Skiing*. Chapter 7, "Working with Images." Pages 93-128.
- Mike Samuels, M.D. & N. Samuels, *Seeing with the Mind's Eye*. Pages 38-73 & 104-133.
- An example of simulation and visualization from the 2010 Winter Olympics in Whistler, BC.

  "The next morning at two and half hours prior to race time, the competitors gathered, in and around the starting hut at the top, for a course ionspection...At nine sharp the official's voice came over a race radio, signalling that the inspection had begun, and the racers, with team warmups and cloaks over their racing suits, began chattering downhill sidewise to the first turn, to see what the next turn looked like from here, and to figure out where they'd want to be to prepare for it. They typically memorize every turn and bump, pausing during their

*inspection to close their eyes and rehearse
the run in their minds, swivelling their hips
and dropping their shoulders to adjust to
imagined contours and curves, in a kind of
Alpine Tai Chi."*

Readings on Relaxation:

- Chungliang Al Huang & J. Lynch, *Thinking Body, Dancing Mind.* Pages 46-51.
- Dalai Lama, *The Art of Happiness.* Pages 246-262.
- Dale Reubart, *Anxiety and Musical Performance.* Pages 137-148.

Readings on Concentration:

- Daniel Goleman, *The Meditative Mind.*
- Eugen Herrigel, *Zen in the Art of Archery.*
- Christmas Humprhies, *Concentration and Meditation.* "Concentration & Exercises in Concentration" Pages 28-52 & 53-66.
- Will Johnson. *The Posture of Meditation: A Practical Manual for Meditators of All Traditions.*
- Lama Surya Das, *Awakening the Buddha Within.* "Right Concentration." Pages 334-395.
- George Leonard, *The Way of Akido.*
- Denise McCluggage, *Centered Skiing.* Chapter 10, "Concentration." Pages 156-173.
- Shunryu Suzuki, *Zen Mind, Beginner's Mind.* "Meditation is not concentration." Pages 136-138.
- Alan Watts, *The Way of Liberation.* "The Practice of Meditation." Pages 91-95.
- Ken Wilber, *The Eye of the Spirit.* Chapter 10.

- Ernest Wood, *Concentration.*

Readings on Mindfulness

- Jon Kabat-Zinn, *Wherever You Go, There You Are.* Pages 3-7
- J. Krishnamurti, *Freedom from the Known.*
- Wes Nicker, *Buddha's Nature.* "Body Scanning." Pages 102-155.
- Wes Nicker, *Buddha's Nature.* "Mindfulness, the Opposable Thumb of Consciousness." Pages 25-30.
- Charles J. Tart, *Living the Mindful Life.*
- Ken Wilber, *The Eye of the Spirit.* Chapter 12.
- Ken Wilber, *The Spectrum of Consciousness.* Chapter 11.
- Ken Wilber, *The Theory of Everything.* Chapter 3.

From *Integral Coaching*

- The collected writings of David Bohm are an important source for integral thought. In particular, *Wholeness and the Implicate Order*, and its opening chapter, *Wholeness and Fragmentation*. It provides insightful perspectives on science, philosophy and life.
- Select works from Georg Feuerstein stand out as crucial pieces for integral thought.
    1. *Lucid Waking: Mindfulness and the Spiritual Potential of Humanity.*
    2. *Structures of Consciousness: The Genius of Jean Gebser.*
- Jean Gebser, *The Ever-Present Origin.*
- *"The old coach skillfully deconstructed the stroke cycle for the young student and the reconstructed the parts back to a logical whole. The observer was witnessing a masterful demonstration reminiscent of a watchmaker reassembling the parts of a delicate timing piece. - Jimmy Joy*
- Krishnamurti and David Bohm, the mystic and the physicist, engaged in numerous dialogues providing many valuable perspectives.
- The foreward of Ken Wilber's *The Eye of the Spirit* by Jack Crittenden titled: "What is the meaning of integral?"

From *Flow*

- David Bohm, *Wholeness and the Implicate Order.*
- F David Peat, Bohm's biographer, wrote in *Infinite Potential: The Life and Times of David Bohm,* the following assessment of a young Bohm: "...a deep transformation had occurred at an inner level. David began to see the world in terms of flows and transformations, processes and movements. No longer would he think of the world exclusively in terms of fixed objects like stones and atoms, for behind them he now saw a previously hidden world of motion and flow." In line with this thinking, coaches have to be aware of a world that is in flux.
- Andrew Cooper, *Playing in the Zone: Exploring the Spiritual Dimension of Sports.*
- Mihaly Csikzentmihalyi, *Flow: The Psychology of Optimal Experience.*
- Susan Jackson & Mihaly Csikzentmihalyi, *Flow in Sports: The Keys to Optimal Experiences and Performance.*
- J. Krishnamurti, *The Wholeness of Life.*
- Abraham Maslow, *Religion, Values and Peak Experience.*
- Michael Murphy, *Golf in the Kingdom.*
- Tony Schwartz, *What Really Matters: Searching for Wisdom in America.*
- A note from Jon Ossowski, Canadian National Team 1983-1987, on his Flow experience.

> *Jim,*
> *Here is a brief recount of one of my most memorable races. I reflect on it often as I try to explain the concept of team to folks who*

haven't had a chance to row, which I think is one of the best learning grounds for what it truly means to be on a team. The situation was as follows: I was the stroke of the National Team Men's 8+ in 1986 and was training out of UVic in Victoria. As it happened, Al Morrow had arranged for us to race Oxford, Cambridge, Harvard, Yale and the Vancouver Rowing Club in the inaugural "Boat Race." Fortunately UVic had a strong university crew that was heavy with National Team members so we were confident on our home course. This was a two day event; Day one was the so called "Cake Race", essentially a 500m sprint in the Inner Harbor. We apparently lost even though most felt the start and finish lines weren't parallel! I started behind the winning boats cox and finished ahead of him, but we still lost. I should mention that we didn't really change any training for this race, e.g., no taper, but in fact looked at it as just another racing workout. It was an overcast day and the pre-race jitters were palpable, but as always when you got in the boat and held on to the oar for a few strokes, your body went to a very familiar place. It is in those first few strokes that I always felt that something switched and magically fear, always turned into excitement. The challenge in this sport is that you want everyone doing the same thing at the same time, the whole crew to feel present and to work together – not fight each other. This is further complicated by the tension between the port and starboard sides who work to achieve lateral balance. Usually when a crew is performing sub-optimally, it is quite clear that they are out of sync and this is often the result of one or two folks desperately trying to make it happen on their own. Refer to the recent Canadian Men's 8+ loss at the recent Olympics were one guy actually lost his slide!!! When I talk about team I use this point to emphasize the need to keep your ego out of the crew as it only screws things up.

The race itself was the standard 2km and as mentioned above there was fair bit of pressure after losing the "cake race" the day before. In addition there were about 10,000 people lining the last 250 meters of the course. Needless to say, the next day the pressure was mounting. I had my trusted friend Eric Kovits behind me in 7-seat and our cox was Brian MacMahon. We did our standard warm-up and as usual I turned to Eric while and said "Lets have some fun!" Things felt great from the first stroke. All of our oars were locked in and there was a satisfying snap in the hull at the end of each stroke as we released the water in unison. After about 10 strokes, 4 seat, occupied by Kevin Neufeld, 1984 Gold medalist, yelled out that our rate was too low and the cox replied back that we were at 43 spm. I think we were all surprised as it didn't feel rushed and yet we were truly accelerating away from the field. I think the message here is that when you have such a great start you do

*your best not to throw things off and too
preserve that feeling. Once we had
established our lead we simply settled into
cruise mode. We were challenged and
always responded together, but never
reacted, it was never frantic. No one over
reached, we stayed within ourselves, and in
other words we preserved the feeling. We
simply established control and rowed our
race, but this curious feeling remained that it
just didn't feel hard! I had had that feeling
before, but it was usually more around the
excitement of knowing that, unless we fell
apart, we were going to win and that always
makes the lactic acid build up less painful.
This time was different though, we truly did
it together. We ended up winning by 4 or 5
seats, but the margin didn't matter, it was
simply how effortless it felt!"*

From the *Summary*

Sugar Ray Robinson was a fluid boxer who commanded a quick jab and knockout power. He possessed tremendous versatility — according to boxing analyst Bert Sugar, "Robinson could deliver a knockout blow going backward." He was efficient with both hands and he displayed a variety of effective punches. TIME magazine, in 1951, cited "Robinson's repertoire, thrown with equal speed and power by either hand, includes every standard punch from a bolo to a hook — and a few he makes up on the spur of the moment. The king, the master, my idol."

- Phil Jackson, *Sacred Hoops*. "The Holzman School of Management." Pages 33-37.
- Shunryu Suzuki, *Zen Mind, Beginner's Mind*. "No Dualism." Pages 41-43.
- Shunryu Suzuki, *Zen Mind, Beginner's Mind*. "Attachment, Non-Attachment." Pages 118-121.
- Charles J. Tart, *Waking Up: Overcoming the Obstacles to Human Potential*. "Balance and Imbalance in Three-Brained Beings." Pages 149-161.
- Ken Wilber, *The Essential Ken Wilber*. "The Non-Dual Vision." Pages 12-15.
- Ken Wilber, *A Theory of Everything: An Integral Vision for Business, Politics, Science and Spirituality*.
- Jean Gebser, *The Ever-Present Origin*. - Take note of Jean Gebser's five stages of cultural development: The archaic, magical, mythical, mental and integral. The magical and integral structures are closest in character to the skills and consciousness of the accomplished athlete.

An excellent introduction to Gebser's book is Feuerstein's *Structures of Conciousness: The Genius of Jean Gebser.*

Joy of Sculling

References

Alexander, F. Matthias. *The Resurrection of the Body.* New York, NY: University Books, 1969.

Aurobindo, Sri. *The Integral Yoga: Sri Aurobindo's Teaching and Method of Practice - Selected Letters of Sri Aurobindo.* Twin Lakes, WI: Lotus Light Publications, 1993.

Bohm, David. *Causality and Chance in Modern Physics.* London, UK: Routledge & Kegan, 1957.

Bohm, David. *Wholeness and the Implicate Order.* New York, NY: Routledge Press, 1980.

Bowerman, William J. *High-Performance Training for Track and Field.* Champaign, IL: Leisure Press, 1991.

Browning, Kurt. 2002.

Bugbee, Henry. *The Inward Morning: A Philosophical Exploration in Journal Form.* Athens, GA: University of Georgia Press, 1999.

Burnell, Richard. *The Oxford Pocket Book of Sculling Training.* London: Oxford University Press, 1962.

Campbell, Neil. Conversation, 1984.

Cerutty, Percy Wells. *Athletics: How to Become a Champion*. London, UK: Stanley Paul, 1960.

Combs, Allan. *The Radiance of Being: Complexity, Chaos, and the Evolution of Consciousness*. St. Paul, MN: Paragon House, 1996.

Csikszentmihalyi, Mihaly. "Play and Intrinsic Rewards." *Journal of Humanistic Psychology* 15, no. 3 (1975).

Daigenault, Ted. Presentations, 1980s.

Dalai, A. S. *Powers Within: Selections from the Works of Sri Aurobindo and the Mother*. Ojai, CA: Institute of Integral Psychology, 2000.

Easwaran, Eknath. *Meditation: A Simple Eight-Point Program for Translating Spiritual Ideals into Daily Life*. 2nd ed. Tomales, CA: Nilgiri Press, 1991.

Elgin, Duane. *Awakening Earth: Exploring the Evolution of Human Culture and Consciousness*. 1st ed. New York, NY: Morrow, 1993.

Elgin, Duane. *The Living Universe: Where Are We? Who Are We? Where Are We Going?* 1st ed. San Francisco, CA: Berrett-Koehler, 2009.

Eliot, T. S. *Four Quartets*. New York, NY: Harcourt, 1943.

Feuerstein, Georg. *Lucid Waking: Mindfulness and the Spiritual Potential of Humanity*. Rochester, VT: Inner Traditions International, 1997.

Feuerstein, Georg. *Structures of Consciousness: The Genius of Jean Gebser-an Introduction and Critique*. Lower Lake, CA: Integral Publishing, 1987.

FISA. "Post-Race Interview with Peter Haining." 1994.

Goleman, Daniel. "Taming Destructive Emotions." *Tricycle*, 2003.

Hanh, Thich Nhat. *Peace Is Every Step: The Path of Mindfulness in Everyday Life*. New York, NY: Bantam Books, 1991.

Hart, Peter. *The Somme: The Darkest Hour on the Western Front*. New York, NY: Penguin Books, 2008.

Heckler, Richard Strozzi. *In Search of the Warrior Spirit: Teaching Awareness Disciplines to the Green Berets*. Berkeley, CA: North Atlantic Books, 2003.

Herrigel, Eugen. *Zen in the Art of Archery*. New York, NY: Vintage Books, 1989.

Huang, Al Chung-liang, and Jerry Lynch. *Thinking Body, Dancing Mind: Taosports for Extraordinary Performance in Athletics, Business and Life*. New York, NY: Bantam Books, 1994.

"Interview with Phil Jackson." USA: CNN, 2002.

Jackson, Phil. *Sacred Hoops: Spiritual Lessons of a Hardwood Warrior*. New York, NY: Hyperion, 1995.

Jackson, Phil, and Charles Rosen. *More Than a Game*. New York, NY: Seven Stories Press, 2001.

Joy, Jimmy. "The Art of Sculling." In *NAAO (Now US Rowing) Annual Meeting*. Syracuse, NY, 1978.

Kelly, F.S. *The Diaries of F.S. Kelly*. Canberra, AUS: National Library of Australia, 2006.

Krishnamurti, J. *The Wholeness of Life*. San Francisco, CA: Harper & Row, 1979.

Leonard, George Burr. *The Transformation: A Guide to the Inevitable Changes in Humankind*. New York, NY: Delacorte Press, 1972.

Liddell-Hart, Basil. *Strategy*. New York, NY: Praeger, 1967.

Mack, William. "The Colossus." *Sports Illustrated*, 1998.

McNeely, Ed. "Integral Coaching." Paper presented at the The Joy of Sculling, Saratoga Springs, NY, 2007.

Merton, Thomas. *The Way of Chuang Tzu*. Boston, MA: Shambhala, 1992.

Ming, Shi. *Mind over Matter: Higher Martial Arts*. Berkeley, CA: North Atlantic Books, 1994.

Mitchell, Stephen. *Tao Te Ching*. New York, NY: Harper, 1988.

Morrow, Al. "Coaching." Paper presented at the The Joy of Sculling, Saratoga, NY, December 2000.

Nisker, Wes. *Buddha's Nature: Evolution as a Practical Guide to Enlightenment*. New York, NY: Bantam Books, 1998.

Page, Geoffrey. *Coaching for Rowing*. London, UK: Museum Press, 1963.

Picard, Max. *The World of Silence*. Wichita, KS: Eighth Day Press, 2002.

Robinson, Sugar Ray, and Dave Anderson. *Sugar Ray: The Sugar Ray Robinson Story*. New York, NY: Viking Press, 1970.

Sanders, Scott Russell. *A Conservationist Manifesto*. Bloomington, IN: Indiana University Press, 2009.

Schmolinsky, Gerhardt, and Deutsche Hochschule für Körperkultur Leipzig. Wissenschaftsbereich Leichtathletik. *Track and Field: Text-Book for Coaches and Sports Teachers*. 1. ed. Berlin: Sportverlag, 1978.

Sheehan, George. *Running and Being: The Total Experience*. New York, NY: Simon and Schuster, 1978.

Tart, Charles J. *Mind Science: Meditation Training for Practical People*. Novato, CA: Wisdom Editions, 2001.

Teilhard de Chardin, Pierre. *The Phenomenon of Man*. New York, NY: Harper, 1959.

Wilber, Ken. *Integral Psychology: Consciousness, Spirit, Psychology, Therapy*. Boston, MA: Shambhala, 2000.

Wilber, Ken. *One Taste: The Journals of Ken Wilber.* Boston, MA: Shambhala, 1999.

Wilber, Ken. *Sex, Ecology, Spirituality: The Spirit of Evolution,* The Collected Works of Ken Wilber. Boston, MA: Shambhala, 2000.

Wing, R. L. . *The Tao of Power.* Garden City, NY: Dolphin Book, 1986.

Bibliography

Abram, David. *The Spell of the Sensuous: Perception and Language in a More Than Human World.* New York, NY: Vintage Books, 1997.

Ackerman, Diane. *Deep Play.* New York, NY: Random House, 1999.

Adler, Mortimer Jerome. *How to Speak, How to Listen.* New York, NY: Macmillan, 1983.

Alexander, Charles Nathaniel, and Ellen J. Langer. *Higher Stages of Human Development: Perspectives on Adult Growth.* New York, NY: Oxford University Press, 1990.

Almaas, A. H. *The Elixir of Enlightenment: The Diamond Approach to Inner Realization.* York Beach, ME: Samuel Weiser, 1984.

Almaas, A. H. *The Pearl Beyond Price: Integration of Personality into Being, an Object Relations Approach.* Berkeley, CA: Diamond Books, 1988.

Almaas, A. H. *The Void: Inner Spaciousness and Ego Structure.* Berkeley, CA: Diamond Books, 1996.

Almaas, A. H. *Elements of the Real in Man.* Boston, MA: Shambhala, 2000.

Assagioli, Roberto. *Psychosynthesis: A Manual of Principles and Techniques.* New York, NY: Hobbs, 1965.

Assagioli, Roberto. *The Act of Will.* New York, NY: Viking Press, 1973.

Bandler, Richard, and John Grinder. *Frogs into Princes: Neuro Linguistic Programming.* Moab, UT: Real People Press, 1979.

Barfield, Owen. *Worlds Apart: A Dialogue of the 1960's.* Middletown, CT: Wesleyan University Press, 1963.

Barlow, Connie C. *Green Space, Green Time: The Way of Science.* New York, NY: Copernicus, 1997.

Beck, Don, and Christopher C. Cowan. *Spiral Dynamics: Mastering Values, Leadership, and*

Change, Developmental Management. Cambridge, MA: Blackwell Business, 1996.

Benoit, Hubert. *The Interior Realization*. York Beach, ME: Samuel Weiser, Inc., 1979.

Benoit, Hubert. *Zen and the Psychology of Transformation: The Supreme Doctrine*. Rochester, VT: Inner Traditions International, 1990.

Benson, Herbert, and William Proctor. *Beyond the Relaxation Response: How to Harness the Healing Power of Your Personal Beliefs*. New York, NY: Times Books, 1984.

Benson, Herbert, and William Proctor. *Your Maximum Mind*. New York, NY: Times Books, 1987.

Berry, Thomas. *The Dream of the Earth*. San Francisco, CA: Sierra Club Books, 1988.

Berry, Wendell. *The Unsettling of America: Culture & Agriculture*. San Francisco, CA: Sierra Club Books, 1986.

Bertherat, Thérèse, and Carol Bernstein. *The Body Has Its Reasons: Self Awareness through Conscious Movement*. Rochester, VT: Healing Arts Press, 1989.

Bohm, David and Peat, F. David. *Science, Order, and Creativity*. London, UK: Routledge, 1987.

Bradley, Bill. *Values of the Game*. New York, NY: Artisan, 1998.

Brunton, Paul. *The Wisdom of the Overself*. London, UK: Rider, 1969.

Bucke, Richard Maurice. *Cosmic Consciousness: A Study in the Evolution of the Human Mind*. Secaucus, NJ: Citadel Press, 1993.

Budbill, David. *Moment to Moment: Poems of a Mountain Recluse*. Port Townsend, WA: Copper Canyon Press, 1999.

Burnell, Richard. *The Complete Sculler*. Toronto, CAN: Sport Books Publisher, 1998.

Cannon, Walter B. *The Wisdom of the Body.* New York, NY: W.W. Norton & Company, 1967.

Castaneda, Carlos. *The Power of Silence: Further Lessons of Don Juan.* New York, NY: Simon and Schuster, 1987.

Cooper, Andrew. *Playing in the Zone: Exploring the Spiritual Dimensions of Sports.* First ed. Boston, MA: Shambhala, 1998.

Cope, Stephen. *Yoga and the Quest for the True Self.* New York, NY: Bantam Books, 1999.

Csikszentmihalyi, Mihaly. *Flow: The Psychology of Optimal Experience.* New York, NY: Harper & Row, 1990.

Custance, Arthur C., and Lee Edward Travis. *The Mysterious Matter of Mind*, Christian Free University Curriculum. Grand Rapids, MI: Zondervan Publishing House, 1980.

Dalai, A. S. *A Greater Psychology: An Introduction to Sri Aurobindo's Psychological Thought.* New York, NY: Putnam, 2001.

Davis, John, and A. H. Almaas. *The Diamond Approach: An Introduction to the Teachings of A.H. Almaas.* 1st ed. Boston, MA: Shambhala, 1999.

Deikman, Arthur. *The Observing Self: Mysticism and Psychotherapy.* Boston, MA: Beacon Press, 1982.

Drucker, Peter F. *The Effective Executive.* 1st ed. New York, NY: Harper & Row, 1967.

Easwaran, Eknath. *Your Life Is Your Message: Finding Harmony with Yourself, Others, & the Earth.* Tomales, CA: Nilgiri Press, 1992.

Eccles, John C., and Daniel N. Robinson. *The Wonder of Being Human: Our Brain and Our Mind.* New York, NY: Random House, 1985.

Elgin, Duane. *Voluntary Simplicity: Toward a Way of Life That Is Outwardly Simple, Inwardly Rich.* 1st ed. New York, NY: Morrow, 1981.

Elgin, Duane. *Promise Ahead: A Vision of Hope and Action for Humanity's Future.* 1st ed. New York: Morrow, 2000.

Emerson, Ralph Waldo, and Henry David Thoreau. *Nature.* Boston, MA: Beacon Press, 1991.

Epstein, Mark. *Thoughts without a Thinker: Psychotherapy from a Buddhist Perspective.* New York, NY: Basic Books, 1995.

Epstein, Mark. *Going to Pieces without Falling Apart: A Buddhist Perspective on Wholeness.* 1st ed. New York, NY: Broadway Books, 1998.

Feldenkrais, Moshé. *Awareness through Movement: Health Exercises for Personal Growth.* 1st ed. San Francisco, CA: Harper, 1990.

Feldenkrais, Moshé, and Michaeleen Kimmey. *The Potent Self: A Guide to Spontaneity.* 1st ed. San Francisco, CA: Harper & Row, 1985.

Feldman, David Henry, Mihaly Csikszentmihalyi, and Howard Gardner. *Changing the World: A Framework for the Study of Creativity.* Westport, CT: Praeger, 1994.

Frankl, Viktor Emil. *Man's Search for Meaning; an Introduction to Logotherapy.* Boston,: Beacon Press, 1963.

Frantzis, Bruce Kumar. *Opening the Energy Gates of Your Body.* Berkeley, CA: North Atlantic Books, 1993.

Freud, Sigmund. *Civilization and Its Discontents.* 1st ed. New York, NY: W. W. Norton, 1962.

Fukuoka, Masanobu. *The Rod Back to Nature: Regaining the Paradise Lost.* Tokyo, Japan: Publications, Inc., 1987.

Gallwey, W. Timothy. *The Inner Game of Tennis.* New York, NY: Random House, 1997.

Gardner, Howard, Mihaly Csikszentmihalyi, and William Damon. *Good Work: When Excellence and Ethics Meet.* New York, NY: Basic Books, 2001.

Gebser, Jean. *The Ever-Present Origin*. Athens, OH: Ohio University Press, 1984.

Gendlin, Eugene T. *Focusing-Oriented Psychotherapy: A Manual of the Experiential Method*. New York, NY: Guilford Press, 1996.

Getzels, Jacob W., and Mihaly Csikszentmihalyi. *Creative Thinking in Art Students: An Exploratory Study*. Chicago, IL: University of Chicago, 1964.

Ghose, Aurobindo. *The Mind of Light*. 1st ed. Twin Lakes, WI: Lotus Press, 2003.

Giono, Jean. *The Man Who Planted Trees*. Chelsea, VT: Chelsea Green Publishing Company, 1985.

Goldsmith, Edward. *The Way: An Ecological World-View*. Athens, GA: University of Georgia Press, 1998.

Goleman, Daniel. *Mindscience: An East-West Dialogue*. Boston, MA: Wisdom Publications, 1991.

Gordon, Mary. *Roots of Empathy: Changing the World, Child by Child*. Toronto, ONT: Thomas Allen Publishers, 2005.

Grahame, Kenneth, and Patrick Benson. *The Wind in the Willows*. New York, NY: St. Martin's Press, 1995.

Grey, Alex. *The Mission of Art*. 1st ed. Boston, MA: Shambhala, 1998.

Grey, Alex, Ken Wilber, and Carlo McCormick. *The Sacred Mirrors: The Visionary Art of Alex Grey*. Rochester, VT: Inner Traditions International, 1990.

Grof, Christina, and Stanislav Grof. *The Stormy Search for the Self: A Guide to Personal Growth through Transformational Crisis*. 1st ed. Los Angeles, CA: St. Martin's Press, 1990.

Hadot, Pierre. *Plotinus, or, the Simplicity of Vision*. Chicago, IL: University of Chicago Press, 1993.

Hadot, Pierre. *Philosophy as a Way of Life*. Malden, MA: Blackwell Publishing, 2006.

Haultain, Arnold. *The Mystery of Golf*. New York, NY: Houghton MIfflin Co., 2000.

Hauser, Thomas.

Hayward, Jeremy W., and Francisco J. Varela. *Gentle Bridges: Conversations with the Dalai Lama on the Sciences of Mind*. Boston, MA: Shambhala Publications, 1992.

Heidegger, Martin. *Being and Time*. London, UK: SCM Press, 1962.

Heider, John. *The Tao of Leadership: Lao Tzu's Tao Te Ching Adapted for a New Age*. Atlanta, GA: Humanics New Age, 1985.

Herrigel, Gustie. *Zen in the Art of Flower Arrangement: An Introduction to the Spirit of the Japanese Art of Flower Arrangement*. Newton Centre, MA: C.T. Branford Co., 1958.

Hesse, Hermann. *The Journey to the East*. London, UK: Grafton Books, 1986.

Hewitt, James. *The Complete Yoga Book: Yoga of Breathing, Yoga of Posture, and Yoga of Meditation*. New York, NY: Schocken Books, 1978.

Hewitt, James. *Relaxation*. Lincolnwood, IL: NTC Pub. Group, 1994.

Howarth, David. *We Die Alone: A Wwii Epic of Escape and Endurance*. Guilford, CT: The Lyons Press, 1999.

Huang, Al Chung-liang, and Jerry Lynch. *Mentoring: The Tao of Giving and Receiving Wisdom*. 1st ed. San Francisco, CA: Harper, 1995.

Huang, Al Chung-liang, and Jerry Lynch. *Working out, Working Within: The Tao of Inner Fitness through Sports and Exercise*. New York, NY: Putnam, 1998.

Hubbard, Harlan. *Payne Hollow: Life on the Fringe of Society*. Frankfort, KY: Gnomon Press, 1974.

Huizinga, Johan. *Homo Ludens: A Study of the Play Element in Culture*. London, UK: Maurice Temple Smith Ltd., 1970.

Humphreys, Christmas. *Concentration and Meditation: A Manual of Mind Development*. Baltimore, MD: Penguin Books, 1970.

Huxley, Aldous. *The Perennial Philosophy*: Harper & Brothers, 1945.

Huxley, Aldous, and Piero Ferrucci. *The Human Situation: Lectures at Santa Barbara, 1959*. London, UK: Chatto & Windus, 1978.

Jackson, Susan A., and Mihaly Csikszentmihalyi. *Flow in Sports*. Champaign, IL: Human Kinetics, 1999.

James, William. *The Varieties of Religious Experience: A Study in Human Nature*. New York, NY: Longmans, Green, and co., 1902.

Johnson, Will. *The Posture of Meditation: A Practical Manual for Meditators of All Traditions*. 1st ed. New York, NY: Shambhala, 1996.

Jung, C. G. *The Undiscovered Self*. 1st ed. Boston, MA: Mentor, 1958.

Kabat-Zinn, Jon. *Wherever You Go, There You Are : Mindfulness Meditation in Everyday Life*. 1st ed. New York: Hyperion, 1994.

Kabat-Zinn, Jon. *Coming to Our Senses: Healing Ourselves and the World through Mindfulness*. New York, NY: Hyperion, 2005.

Keen, Sam. *Learning to Fly: Trapeze--Reflections on Fear, Trust, and the Joy of Letting Go*. 1st ed. New York, NY: Broadway Books, 1999.

Keen, Sam. *Sightings: Extraordinary Encounters with Ordinary Birds*. San Francisco, CA: Chronicle Books, 2007.

Kegan, Robert. *The Evolving Self: Problem and Process in Human Development*. Cambridge, MA: Harvard University Press, 1982.

Kegan, Robert. *In over Our Heads: The Mental Demands of Modern Life.* Cambridge, MA: Harvard University Press, 1994.

King, Ursula. *The Spirit of One Earth: Reflections on Teilhard De Chardin and Global Spirituality.* New York, NY: Paragon House, 1989.

Kingsley, Peter. *Ancient Philosophy, Myster, and Magic: Empedocles and Pythagorean Tradition.* Oxford, UK: Clarendon Press, 1995.

Kingsley, Peter. *In Dark Places of Wisdom.* Inverness, CA: The Golden Sufi Center, 2004.

Kleinman, Seymour. *Mind and Body: East Meets West,* Big Ten Body of Knowledge Symposium Series V. 15. Champaign, IL: Human Kinetics, 1986.

Koestler, Arthur. *The Ghost in the Machine.* 1st ed. New York, NY: Random House, 1982.

Krishnamurti, J. *Education and the Significance of Life.* New York, NY: Harper, 1953.

Krishnamurti, J. *The First and Last Freedom.* New York, NY: Harper & Row, 1975.

Krishnamurti, J. *Meeting Life: Writings and Talks on Finding Your Path without Retreating from Society.* San Francisco, CA: Harper, 1991.

Krishnamurti, J. *Freedom, Love, and Action.* Boston, MA: Shambhala, 1994.

Krishnamurti, J. *On Learning and Knowledge.* San Francisco, CA: Harper, 1994.

Krishnamurti, J. *This Light in Oneself: True Meditation.* Boston, MA: Shambhala, 1999.

Krishnamurti, J., and Mary Lutyens. *Freedom from the Known.* London, UK: Gollancz, 1969.

Lama, Dalai. *The Art of Happiness: A Handbook for Living.* New York, NY: Riverhead Books, 1998.

Lama, Dalai. *The Universe in a Single Atom: The Convergence of Science and Spirituality.* New York, NY: Morgan Road Books, 2005.

Lambert, Craig. *Mind over Water: Lessons on Life from the Art of Rowing.* Boston, MA: Houghton Mifflin Co., 1998.

Langer, Ellen J. *Mindfulness.* Cambridge, MA: Perseus Books, 1989.

Leonard, George Burr. *The Ultimate Athlete: Re-Visioning Sports, Physical Education, and the Body.* New York, NY: Viking Press, 1975.

Leonard, George Burr. *Mastery: The Keys to Long-Term Success and Fulfillment.* New York, NY: Dutton, 1991.

Leonard, George Burr. *The Way of Aikido: Life Lessons from an American Sensei.* New York, NY: Dutton, 1999.

Leopold, Aldo. *A Sand County Almanac and Sketches Here and There.* Oxford, UK: Oxford University Press, 1987.

Leopold, Aldo. *For the Health of the Land.* Washington, DC: Island Press, 1999.

LeShan, Lawrence L. *How to Meditate: A Guide to Self-Discovery.* Boston, MA: Bantam Books, 1974.

Levey, Joel, and Michelle Levey. *Living in Balance: A Dynamic Approach for Creating Harmony and Wholeness in a Chaotic World.* Berkeley, CA: Conari Press, 1998.

Liao, Waysun. *The Essence of T'ai Chi.* Boston, MA: Shambhala, 1995.

Livingston, Michael K. *Mental Discipline: The Pursuit of Peak Performance.* Champaign, IL: Human Kinetics, 1989.

Lowe, Benjamin. *The Beauty of Sport: A Cross-Disciplinary Inquiry.* Englewood Cliffs, NJ: Prentice-Hall, 1977.

Lydiard, Arthur, and Garth Gilmour. *Distance Training for Young Athletes.* Aachen: Meyer and Meyer Sport, 1999.

Martin, Roger H. *Racing Odysseus: A College President Becomes a Freshman Again*. Berkeley, CA: University of California, 2008.

Maslow, Abraham H. *Religions, Values, and Peak-Experiences*. Columbus, OH: Ohio State University, 1964.

McCluggage, Denise. *The Centered Skier*. New York, NY: Bantam Books, 1983.

Merton, Thomas. *Mystics and Zen Masters*. New York, NY: Farrar, 1967.

Muktananda, Swami. *Meditate*. Albany, NY: State University of New York, 1980.

Murphy, Michael. *The Future of the Body: Explorations into the Further Evolution of Human Nature*. Los Angeles, CA: Tarcher, 1992.

Murphy, Michael. *Golf in the Kingdom*. New York, NY: Penguin, 1997.

Nairn, Rob. *Diamond Mind: A Psychology of Meditation*. Boston, MA: Shambhala, 1999.

Nansen, Fritdjof. *Farthest North: The Incredible Three-Year Voyage to the Frozen Latitudes of the North*. New York, NY: Modern Library, 1999.

Nasr, Seyyed Hossein. *Religion & the Order of Nature*. New York, NY: Oxford University Press, 1996.

Needleman, Jacob. *A Sense of the Cosmos: Scientific Knowledge and Spiritual Truth*. Rhinebeck, NY: Monkfish Book Publishing Co., 1975.

Nietzsche, Friedrich Wilhelm. *The Portable Nietzsche*. New York, NY: Penguin Books, 1976.

Osho. *Gold Nuggets*. Cologne, Germany: Rebel Press, 1988.

Osho. *The Everyday Meditation*. Boston: Tuttle Co, 1993.

Osho. *What Is Meditation?* Rockport, MA: Element, 1995.

Osho. *Awareness: The Key to Living in Balance*. New York, NY: St. Martin's Press, 2001.

Osho, Wadud Deva, and Svarup Anand. *Meditation: The First and Last Freedom*. Poona, India: Rebel Press, 1992.

Osho, Priya Krishna, and Paras Prem. *The Empty Boat: Talks on the Stories of Chuang Tzu*. Poona, India: Rajneesh Foundation, 1976.

Palmer, Parker J. *The Courage to Teach: Exploring the Inner Landscape of a Teacher's Life*. San Francisco, CA: Jossey-Bass, 1998.

Palmer, Parker J. *The Active Life: A Spirituality of Work, Creativity, and Caring*. San Francisco, CA: Jossey-Bass, 1999.

Palmer, Parker J. *Let Your Life Speak: Listening for the Voice of Vocation*. San Francisco, CA: Jossey-Bass, 2000.

Palmer, Wendy. *The Intuitive Body: Aikido as a Clairsentient Practice*. Berkeley, CA: North Atlantic Books, 1994.

Pearce, Joseph Chilton. *The Crack in the Cosmic Egg: Challenging Constructs of Mind and Reality*. New York, NY: Julian Press, 1971.

Pearce, Joseph Chilton. *Exploring the Crack in the Cosmic Egg: Split Minds and Meta-Realities*. New York, NY: Julian Press, 1974.

Pearce, Joseph Chilton. *Magical Child: Rediscovering Nature's Plan for Our Children*. New York, NY: Dutton, 1977.

Peat, F. David. *Infinite Potential: The Life and Times of David Bohm*. Reading, MA: Helix Books, 1997.

Peat, F. David. *Blackfoot Physics: A Journey into the Native American Universe*. Grand Rapids, MI: Phanes Press, 2002.

Pelletier, Kenneth R. *Mind as Healer, Mind as Slayer: A Holistic Approach to Preventing Stress Disorders*. New York, NY: Delacorte Press/S. Lawrence, 1977.

Penfield, Wilder. *The Mystery of the Mind: A Critical Study of Consciousness and the Human Brain*.

Princeton, NJ: Princeton University Press, 1975.

Plotinus. *The Enneads*. Burdett, NY: Larsen Press, 1992.

Raine, Kathleen. *The Inner Journey of the Poet*. New York, NY: George Braziller, 1982.

Ralston, Peter, and Cheng Hsin. *The Principles of Effortless Power*. Berkely, CA: North Atlantic Books, 1989.

Reubart, Dale. *Anxiety and Musical Performance: On Playing the Piano from Memory*. New York, NY: Da Capo Press, 1985.

Richards, Mary Caroline. *Centering in Pottery, Poetry, and the Person*. 2nd ed. Middletown, CT: Wesleyan University Press, 1989.

Samuels, Mike, and Nancy Samuels. *Seeing with the Mind's Eye: The History, Techniques, and Uses of Visualization*. New York, NY: Random House, 1975.

Sanders, Scott Russell. *Writing from the Center*. Bloomington, IN: Indiana University Press, 1997.

Sanders, Scott Russell. *The Force of Spirit*. Boston, MA: Beacon press, 2000.

Satprem. *Sri Aurobindo, or, the Adventure of Consciousness*. New York, NY: Institute for Evolutionary Research, 1984.

Scaravelli, Vanda. *Awakening the Spine: The Stress-Free New Yoga That Works with the Body to Restore Health, Vitality, and Energy*. San Francisco, CA: Harper, 1991.

Schultz, Lucas Estrella. *The Path of the Warrior*. New York: St. Martin's Press, 1998.

Schumacher, E. F. *Small Is Beautiful: Economics as If People Mattered*. London, UK: Harper & Row, 1973.

Schumacher, E. F. *A Guide for the Perplexed*. 1st ed. New York, NY: Harper & Row, 1977.

Schwartz, Tony. *What Really Matters: Searching for Wisdom in America*. New York, NY: Bantam Books, 1995.

Selye, Hans. *The Stress of Life*. New York, NY: McGraw-Hill, 1978.

Seneca. *Letters from a Stoic*. Baltimore, MD: Penguin Books, 1969.

Sherrington, Charles Scott. *Man on His Nature*. Cambridge, UK: Cambridge University Press, 1940.

Shoemaker, Fred, and Pete Shoemaker. *Extraordinary Golf: The Art of the Possible*. New York, NY: Putnam, 1996.

Sinetar, Marsha. *Ordinary People as Monks and Mystics: Lifestyles for Self-Discovery*. New York, NY: Paulist Press, 1986.

Skolimowski, Henryk. *The Participatory Mind: A New Theory of Knowledge and of the Universe*. New York, NY: Penguin Books, 1994.

Smith, Huston. *Beyond the Post-Modern Mind*. Wheaton, IL: Theosophical Publishing House, 1989.

Smith, Huston. *Forgotten Truth: The Common Vision of the World's Religions*. San Francisco, CA: Harper, 1992.

Smith, Huston. *Why Religion Matters: The Fate of the Human Spirit in an Age of Disbelief*. New York, NY: Harper Collins, 2001.

Spicker, Stuart F. *The Philosophy of the Body; Rejections of Cartesian Dualism*. Chicago,: Quadrangle Books, 1970.

Steiner, Rudolf. *Intuitive Thinking as a Spiritual Path*. New York, NY: Anthroscopic Press, 1995.

Stevens, John. *Dewdrops on a Lotus Leaf: Zen Poems of Ryokan*. Boston, MA: Shambhala, 1993.

Stevens, John. *One Robe, One Bowl: The Zen Poetry of Ryokan*. Boston, MA: Weatherhill, 2006.

Strunk, William, and E. B. White. *The Elements of Style*. 4th ed. Boston, MA: Allyn and Bacon, 1999.

Surya, Das. *Awakening the Buddha Within: Eight Steps to Enlightenment - Tibetan Wisdom for the Western World*. New York, NY: Broadway Books, 1997.

Suzuki, Daisetz Teitaro. *The Zen Doctrine of No-Mind: The Significance of the Sutra of Hui-Neng*. London, UK: Rider, 1969.

Suzuki, Shunry u, and Trudy Dixon. *Zen Mind, Beginner's Mind*. 1st ed. New York, NY: Weatherhill, 1970.

Syer, John. *Team Spirit: The Elusive Experience*. London, UK: Kingswood Press, 1986.

Takuan, Soho, and William Scott Wilson. *The Unfettered Mind: Writings of the Zen Master to the Sword Master*. New York, NY: Harper & Row, 1986.

Tart, Charles J. *Mindfulness: Meditation Training for Practical People*. Novata, CA: Wisdom Editions, 2001.

Tart, Charles T. *Waking Up: Overcoming the Obstacles to Human Potential*. 1st ed. New York, NY: Random House, 1986.

Tart, Charles T. *Living the Mindful Life*. 1st ed. Boston & New York: Shambhala: Distributed by Random House, 1994.

Teilhard de Chardin, Pierre. *The Making of a Mind: Letters from a Soldier-Priest, 1914-1919*. New York, NY: Harper & Row, 1965.

Teilhard de Chardin, Pierre. *The Future of Man*. New York, NY: Doubleday, 2004.

Thoreau, Henry David. *Walden and Civil Disobedience*. Ann Arbor, MI: Borders, 2006.

Thoreau, Henry David, and Bruce Rogers. *Walking*. Cambridge, MA: The Riverside Press, 1914.

Todd, Mabel Elsworth. *The Thinking Body: A Study of the Balancing Forces of Dynamic Man.* Brooklyn, NY: Dance Horizons, 1968.

Trungpa, Chogyam, and Carolyn Rose Gimian. *Shambhala: The Sacred Path of the Warrior.* Boston, MA: Shamhala, 1988.

Trungpa, Chogyam, and Judith L. Lief. *Training the Mind & Cultivating Loving-Kindness.* Boston, MA: Shambhala, 1993.

Tzu, Sun. *The Art of War*1971.

Vaughan, Frances E. *Shadows of the Sacred: Seeing through Spiritual Illusions.* Wheaton, IL: Quest Books, 1995.

von Goethe, Johann Wolfgang. *The Metamorphosis of Plants.* Cambridge, MA: MIT Press, 2009.

Wade, Jenny. *Changes of Mind: A Holonomic Theory of the Evolution of Consciousness.* Albany, NY: State University of New York Press, 1996.

Wallace, B. Alan. *The Taboo of Subjectivity: Toward a New Science of Consciousness.* Oxford, UK: Oxford University Press, 2000.

Wallace, B. Alan. *The Attention Revolution: Unlocking the Power of the Focused Mind.* 1st Wisdom ed. Boston: Wisdom Publications, 2006.

Wallace, B. Alan. *Balancing the Mind: A Tibetan Buddhist Approach to Refining Attention.* Ithaca, NY: Snow Lion, 2006.

Wallace, B. Alan. *Contemplative Science: Where Buddhism and Neuroscience Converge.* New York, NY: Columbia University Press, 2007.

Walton, Gary M. *Beyond Winning: The Timeless Wisdom of Great Philosopher Coaches.* Champaign, IL: Leisure Press, 1992.

Watts, Alan. *Still the Mind: An Introduction to Meditation.* Novato, CA: New World Library, 2000.

Watts, Alan, Mark Watts, and Rebecca Shropshire. *The Way of Liberation: Essays and Lectures on*

the Transformation of the Self. New York, NY:
Weatherhill, 1983.

Weil, Thomas E. *Reflections on a Tradition: English
and American Rowing Art.* Washington, DC:
Georgetown University Press, 1990.

Weiss, Paul. *Sport: A Philosophic Inquiry.* Carbondale,
IL: Southern Illinois University Press, 1969.

Wilber, Ken. *The Spectrum of Consciousness,* Quest
Books. Wheaton, IL: Theosophical Publishing
House, 1993.

Wilber, Ken. *The Eye of Spirit: An Integral Vision for a
World Gone Slightly Mad.* Boston, MA:
Shambhala, 1997.

Wilber, Ken. *The Essential Ken Wilber: An Introductory
Reader.* Boston, MA: Shambhala, 1998.

Wilber, Ken. *The Collected Works of Ken Wilber.*
Boston, MA: Shambhala, 1999.

Wilber, Ken. *A Theory of Everything: An Integral Vision
for Business, Politics, Science, and Spirituality.*
Boston, MA: Shambhala, 2000.

Wilber, Ken. *Eye to Eye: The Quest for the New
Paradigm.* Boston, MA: Shambhala, 2001.

Wilber, Ken. *Quantum Questions: Mystical Writings of
the World's Great Physicists.* Boston, MA:
Shambhala, 2001.

Wilson, Colin. *Access to Inner Worlds.* London, UK:
Rider & Co. , 1983.

Wilson, Edward O. *Biophilia: The Human Bond with
Other Species.* Cambridge, MA: Harvard
University Press, 1984.

Wilson, Edward O. *The Creation: An Appeal to Save
Life on Earth.* New York, NY: W. W. Norton &
Co. , 2006.

Wilson, Frank R. *Tone Deaf and All Thumbs?: An
Invitation to Music-Making.* New York, NY:
Vintage Books, 1987.

Wolf, Fred Alan. *The Body Quantum: The New Physics of Body, Mind, and Health.* New York, NY: Macmillan, 1986.

Wood, Ernest. *Concentration.* London: Quest, 1994.

2112854R00082

Printed in Great Britain
by Amazon.co.uk, Ltd.,
Marston Gate.